Dilho

GW00674400

A History of the Parish and its People

Kevin Salt M.A.

CHURNET VALLEY BOOKS
1 King Street, Leek, Staffordshire. ST13 5NW 01538 399033
www.leekbooks.co.uk
© Kevin Salt and Churnet Valley Books 2013
ISBN 9781904546900

ACKNOWLEDGEMENTS

Most communities today, no matter how large or small, have some form of local history published, either in book form or on the web. Dilhorne, however, appeared to be one of those rare exceptions.

The initial intention began as a genealogical project when tracing my own family history. While searching through the parish and manorial records for my Salt ancestors from Dilhorne it became apparent that their names would be more meaningful if set against the context in which they existed. Therefore the work became more of a local, rather than family, history. Local and family history is often segregated. In this book I hope I have demonstrated how the two are, and always should be, inextricably linked.

I am grateful to the following for their help in the preparation of this book: Paul Adams, Matthew Blake, Susan Mace (nee Stevenson), Marcia Curl (nee Salt), Michael Faulkner, Aubrey Salt, Audrey Salt, Wendy Salt, and Mum and Dad.

Kevin Salt

Kevin Salt spent his childhood in the neighbouring community of Blythe Bridge within the ancient parish of Dilhorne, He studied local history at Keele University and obtained a Certificate of Education and a Masters degree in the subject. He also has a Diploma in Archives and Records Management from Liverpool University. He has worked at the Wedgwood Museum, Staffordshire County Record Office and Shugborough Hall.

Bibliography

Beaver, Stanley H., Village Facilities Survey, Community Council of Staffordshire, 1983.

Chester, Herbert A. *Cheadle Coal Town,* Self-published, 1981.

Finn, *Possessions and Place in a Rural Community.*

Griffith, George*, Free Schools and Endowments of Staffordshire*, Whittaker and Co., London, 1860.

Horn, Pamela, *The Victorian Country Child*, Alan Sutton, 1974.

Mingay, G.E., *Rural Life in Victorian England*, Sutton, 1976, revised edition, 1998.

Nichols, Isobel. *The Monumental Inscriptions of All Saints Church*, Dilhorne.

Pevsner., Nicholas. *The Buildings of Staffordshire.* Yale

Pitt, William, *Topographical History of Staffordshire* 1817.

Pointon, Matthew E., *A History of the Parish of Draycott-en-le-Moors*, Draycott Parish Council, 2006.

Rogers, Mike, *The Spirit of the Place*, Three Shires, revised edition, 2000.

Rowley, Trevor, *Villages in the Landscape*, Orion, 1994.

Short, George W. *The Staffordshire Moorlands Volume 1*, Brampton Publications, 1988.

Standley, A. J., *Stafford Gaol. A Chronological Story*. Typed Mss. Stafford WSL.

Walton, Cathryn and Porter, Lindsey, *Lost Houses of North Staffordshire*. Landmark 2006.

Williams, John, The Dilhorne Chronicles, a series of reminiscences that appeared in *The Post and Times* in 1994, March 10th (p13); March 31st (p10); April 7th (p4); April 14th (p14); April 21st (p6).

Staffordshire Weekly Sentinel, April 27 1973, p6. Focus on Folk *Where the Iron Horse is Still Cherished.*

CONTENTS

The author sketching Dilhorne Church, July 3rd, 1971.

INTRODUCTION

Dilhorne has probably never looked as green as it does in the 21st century. The evidence of mining, from which the community took its name has now all but disappeared under grass. Today one would have to look hard for the remains of the collieries or open cast workings, or the tramways that were constructed, along with other signs of industrial activity.[1]

Dilhorne is a prime example of demonstrating the misconception that the countryside does not change. This is also true of the settlements they contain. Trevor Rowley in his classic study *Villages in the Landscape* succinctly noted that settlements, like the people who live in them, are mortal.[2] The notable difference is that people have a predictable life-span which cannot be applied to settlements. However, settlements are never static, often growing, sometimes declining, and constantly changing shape as they respond and adapt to both internal and external factors. It is these events which determine their life-span.

The settlement of Dilhorne lies in the ancient parish of the same name, six miles from the industrial heartland of the Potteries and two miles from the market town of Cheadle. The parish also contained the township of Forsbrook, along with numerous outlying farmsteads, until 1849 when a chapel of ease was built at Forsbrook and its own ecclesiastical parish formed.[3]

The name originates from Dulverne, meaning a place of digging or delving, while Fotesbroc refers to the brook that runs through the centre of the settlement. Dilhorne could be described as a linear village, that is, one which developed along a stretch of road rather than having a central focal point. Forsbrook, on the other hand, could be considered a square village, its nucleus being at the junction of three roads around which the village square developed.

The linear shape of the settlement appears to have been determined by the topography. The area around the church offered a small ridge of flat, dry land with the natural resources of arable-and grazing land, with woodland and water nearby. Close to the church a group of dwellings would have huddled together for security from both man and beast. This may have extended in a northerly direction to where the Hall would be built and onto what would later become the junction of the High Street and the Common.

Alternatively this later area may have developed as a separate community, slowly expanding as the dwellings around the church did. A natural area of lowland separates these two areas. Of the two it appears more probable that the original settlement was that centred around the church. The area around Godley Brook no doubt developed separately from both of these linked only by their inclusion in the same parish and township. However to the casual visitor all three of these areas today would be regarded as Dilhorne.

Equally it is just as difficult to be precise about the outlying hamlets such as Blythe Marsh, Boundary and Whitehurst. These may have developed at the same time or have been emigration from the original settlement. All three of the separate settlements appear to have grown piecemeal with little evidence of regulated planning, emphasised by the vast differences in tenement boundaries.

Footnotes

1. With the exception of The Foxfield Colliery whose railway line is preserved as a tourist attraction.
2. Rowley, Trevor, 'Village in the Landscape', p2.
3. Although the ecclesiastical parish was formed in 1849 Forsbrook did not achieve civil parish status until the changes brought about by the Local Government Act of 1894.

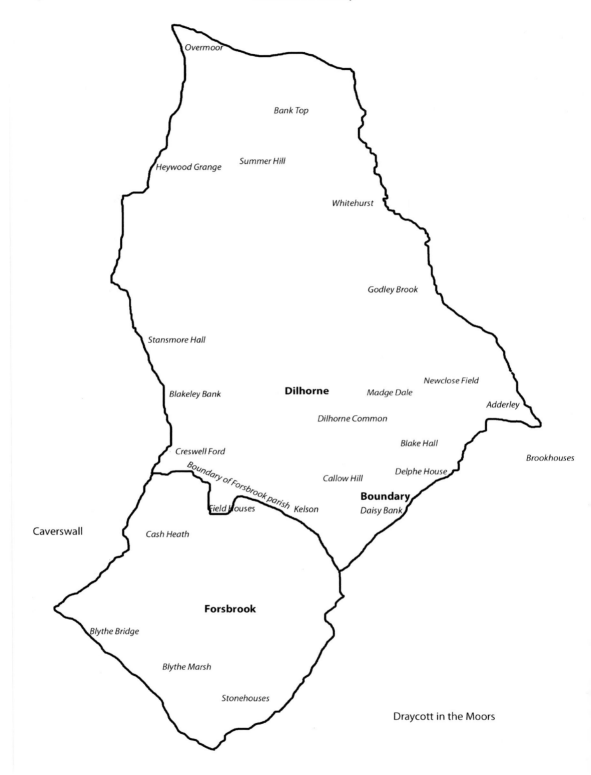

Overmoor

Bank Top

Summer Hill

Heywood Grange

Whitehurst

Godley Brook

Stansmore Hall

Newclose Field

Dilhorne

Madge Dale

Blakeley Bank

Adderley

Dilhorne Common

Blake Hall

Brookhouses

Creswell Ford

Delphe House

Boundary of Forsbrook parish

Callow Hill

Boundary

Field Houses

Kelson

Daisy Bank

Caverswall

Cash Heath

Forsbrook

Blythe Bridge

Blythe Marsh

Stonehouses

Draycott in the Moors

PARISH MAP.

1. The Anglo-Saxon Settlement

That Dilhorne appears in the Domesday Book of 1086 suggests that the community was established during the Anglo-Saxon period. The location may have been the choice of a thane who wanted to establish a homestead and to cultivate enough land for the sustenance of his own household. Alternatively Dilhorne may even have its origins in the Iron or Bronze Age as the plentiful supply of coal would have provided fuel for the early furnaces. Without the evidence of archaeology it is impossible to be precise about the conception of the community, using only the few visible clues on the ground rather than what may lie beneath.

One of these early settlers gave their name to Callow Hill Lane. The name 'Low' often denotes a burial mound and its location on higher ground at a respectable distance from the community suggests that this was the resting place of a tribal leader, possibly the person who founded the settlement.[4] Who he was is unknown, except that his name would have begun with the typical Saxon 'Ca' in the same way that an individual called Cafhere gave his name to nearby Cafhere's Well, which has mutated through time into Caverswall. Alternatively, the name may have originated from the Old English 'Calu' meaning bald. At the time of the burial this high spot above the community may have been bare of trees. Also at the end of Callow Hill Lane is the area known as St Thomas's Trees. This large raised almost circular area is thought to be the site of an ancient settlement and during the 1920s a number of Roman coins were discovered on the site.[5] This suggests that some form of habitation in the area had taken place before the Romans departed Britain in 410.

The houses of the Anglo-Saxon settlement would have consisted of a wooden frame in-filled with wattle and daub, being a mixture of clay, straw and cow-dung. As well as the door the small windows were fitted with wattle shutters to help protect against the elements, and the structure thatched with straw or reeds. In the centre of the earth floor was the hearth providing heat for both cooking and warmth. Sanitation consisted of cess pits outside.

The sound of the community was that of birds, the splash of the watermill, the rumble and creak of a cart travelling along the lane, the wheeze of the blacksmiths bellows and hammer striking anvil. Standing above the village in the area of St Thomas's Trees the view would not have been very different from that of today. It is largely a myth that England at this time was excessively wooded. Clearances of woodland had begun around 5000BC during the Neolithic Period and had steadily continued as wood was both fuel and building materials. Although still revered as the home of ancient spirits woodlands were also a place of employment for coppicing and charcoal burning, as well as feeding swine. With the exception of fields that were later sub-divided most of the patterns in today's landscape would have been recognisable even then.

The inhabitants were practical people who learnt their tasks from their fathers. Dressed in tunics and leggings, with cloaks for colder weather, the majority would have been what is thought of today as peasants. The term peasant is used as an umbrella for the working class when most of this social group were composed of farm labourers. During the Anglo-Saxon period these were known as serfs although the terms bordar, or villein for the more affluent, were used after the Norman Conquest. Naturally many other working class occupations including bakers, millers and blacksmiths were also in existence. Boys aged twelve were deemed mature enough to be adults, while those over fifty were revered as the elders of the community. They would have known everybody, and everybody's business, as the settlement would have been the limit of their lives. Some would have known people in neighbouring settlements and a few would have travelled to the embryonic market town of Cheadle.

Life was regulated by the months of the year. Ploughing would begin in January, followed by pruning and weed-clearing in February, before planting seeds in March. Sheep-shearing would occur in May, with the fleeces then washed and combed before spinning. In July reaping hay would take place to provide winter food for the livestock, followed by harvesting in August.

At the end of the day the household would have gathered around the central fire to enjoy storytelling, the main form of entertainment. This ranged from their own family histories which could stretch back many generations, to epic sagas such as Beowulf. Equally popular were evenings of guessing riddles.

> Head down, nosing-I belly the ground
> Hard snuffle and grub, I bite and furrow
> Drawn by the dark enemy of forests,
> Driven by a bent lord who hounds my trail,
> Who lifts and lowers me, rams me down,
> Pushes on plain, and sows seed.
> I am a ground-skulker, born of wood
> Bound by wizards, brought on wheel
> My ways are weird: as I walk one flank
> of my trail is gathering green, the other
> is bright black. Through my back and belly
> a sharp sword thrusts; through my head
> a dagger is stuck like a tooth: what I slash
> falls in a curve of slaughter to one side
> if my driving lord slaves well.[6]

Bread was the staple diet, although during the Anglo-Saxon period this was very different from that of today. It was a flat round loaf with a heavy texture usually made from wheat, although barley or rye would also be used in times of hardship. Mutton and pork were by far the most common meats consumed, while beef was considered a delicacy. Poultry was venerated as having healing properties and largely reserved for those who were sick.

Starvation was common, especially during late summer before the food harvest was gathered in and which was referred to as the hungry gap. With the exception of the wealthy, many people would have been light-headed for much of the time through lack of food. People would eat berries, acorns and even grasses as an extreme. Hedgerow herbs would have supplemented the dwindling stocks of flour, including poppies, hemp and darnel. The ergot that floured on rye as it grew mouldy was a source of lysergic acid, unbeknown until the 1960s as LSD, although producing the same effects. All of these during times of hardship would have been dried and ground and used in bread making the Hungry Gap more bearable.

Footnotes

4. The mound lies immediately to the west of St Thomas's Trees. It should not be confused with the small flat-topped mound with a shallow ditch around its circumference that lies immediately east of St Thomas's Trees which appears to be the remains of later industrial activity.

5. This was excavated by the Stoke on Trent Museum Archaeological Society. North Staffordshire Field Club Transactions, 1987, p25. NSFCT, 1983, p13.

6. One such example may have been 'Riddle 19' found in the 10th century anthology of Anglo-Saxon poetry known as 'The Exeter Book': The answer is a plough.

2. Domesday

The large circular mound at St Thomas's Trees.

The first documentary evidence of a settlement at Dilhorne is, like so many other places, its existence in the Domesday Book. However, it should be mentioned that entries in Domesday refer not to settlements but to manors. It was only with the Norman Conquest that all the land in England belonged to the King. Previously the tribal mentality of the Anglo-Saxons meant that land belonged to the community that occupied it, divided between the families on the condition of fines and dues payable to the local chief, a position that evolved into the Lord of the Manor.

Had it not have been for the threat of a Scandinavian invasion in 1085 the Domesday Book would not have been compiled. William, who had now been King of England for nearly twenty years, needed to raise and finance a large mercenary army to defend his kingdom. Thus began a long tradition of when a king needed money for war the best way to accomplish this, through his eyes, was by taxation. However this was not completely new as Alfred the Great had previously used the same method when raising Danegeld in an attempt to pacify earlier invaders.

Domesday, therefore, is a taxation list, based on what was known as the hide. This was the equivalent of 120 acres, not necessarily actual acreage on the ground, but as a unit for taxation purposes. Because the hide was a relatively large area it was commonly divided into four virgates, each virgate representing approximately thirty acres. Like hides, in many cases this did not relate to physical acreage, but again an equivalent for taxation. Dilhorne, along with the neighbouring estates of Caverswall and Cheadle (Draycott was not included in the survey), were each valued at one virgate although in reality each may have differed vastly in size.

Before the Conquest the Manor of Dilhorne was held by a free man called Goduin along with two other free men. This is the only reference to who governed the settlement at the close of the Anglo-Saxon period. By the time of Domesday William had granted the Manor to Robert de Stafford, the younger son of Roger de Toni who had been William's standard bearer at the battle of Hastings. Robert was a prominent landowner with numerous estates in Staffordshire and so he sub-let many of his Manors, with Dilhorne granted to an individual called Walter.

It is a misconception that the original pre-Conquest landowners were dispossessed of their property shortly after the Conquest. This only occurred to those who were killed at Hastings or who had fought against William. The majority of Staffordshire landowners such as Goduin were not ejected from their estates until after twice rebelling against William during 1069 and 1070. Indeed, the Conquest, or the Battle of Hastings, was probably not even heard of in Dilhorne until a week or so later, so poor were the conditions of the roads. Even so, battles were taking place all of the time. This was just another skirmish, even though the king had been killed, miles away on the south coast. The full reciprocations of the Conquest would not be felt for another three or four years. For most people the Conquest would have been hardly noticeable with the exception of a new Lord of the Manor. Life continued at a local level similar to before.

The one virgate of land at Dilhorne contained an acre of meadow along with woodland two leagues in length and a league wide. Woodland was included in the assessment because it contributed to the overall value of the estate by providing building materials, fuel and pannage. Entries were always recorded as being x in length by y in breadth, although this should not be taken that the landscape was covered in a pattern of rectangular woodlands. There was enough land for four ploughs, this information being recorded because wealth was based upon land, and how the profitability of land could be increased. Land in demesne, that is land farmed directly by the Lord of the Manor, was half a plough. The five villeins and five bordars resident on the Manor possessed three-and-a-half ploughs. The half plough owned by the Lord of the Manor was probably one which was shared with one belonging to the other tenants. The total of four matching the land that was available for ploughing suggests that the estate was being farmed to capacity. The whole Manor was valued at twenty shillings, the amount of income the Lord could expect to receive annually if the estate was let for rent.

Forsbrook, which was still in the possession of the King, had enough land for one plough although it was regarded as waste. Many entries in Staffordshire were recorded likewise, or as having a proportion that was waste. Like woodland, this was also a valuable commodity in agriculture for the pasturing of livestock and coppicing. The fact that waste was not recorded in either Dilhorne, Caverswall or Cheadle suggests that much of the land was already being exploited. No other details are recorded for Forsbrook other than before the Conquest it had been held by an individual called Suuain.

By comparison the neighbouring Manor of Caverswall was in possession of Robert de Stafford, who in turn sub-let it to Ernulf de Hesding. Before the Conquest it had been held by a free man called Ulviet who also held Tean with an individual called Ulmer.[7] Like Dilhorne the one virgate had enough land for four ploughs. There were ten villeins and two bordars with three ploughs and in demesne was one further plough. There was six acres of meadow and woodland one league long and half a league wide. It was worth thirty shillings, this higher valuation probably due to a combination of a greater area of meadow and the unusual entry recording half the church of Stoche [Stoke] as having half a carucate of land.[8]

Cheadle was also held by Robert de Stafford, who had sub-let the Manor to another called Robert. Before the Conquest this had been in the possession of a free woman called Godeva.[9] Here the one virgate of land, like Dilhorne and Caverswall, could support four ploughs. There were seven villeins and one bordar with one and a half ploughs and in demesne was one other plough. The fact that only two and a half ploughs were working on land that was capable of accommodating four suggests that some economic misfortune had recently occurred. Like

The view looking south-west from St Thomas's Trees.

Dilhorne the Manor also contained an acre of meadow and woodland two leagues in length and a league wide, and similarly was valued at twenty shillings. There was also a mill that rendered 12d. annually. Although buildings were not normally listed in Domesday, mills were an exception as they produced revenue, the Lord charging a fee for its use.

With the figures stated for the number of villeins and bordars for these manors it is possible to provide the first population estimates. Villeins were prominent and important tenants of the Lord of the Manor, usually with a large household and with dependant labourers of their own. Bordars had a smaller share of the resources and generally smaller households. Taking into

The view from near St Thomas's Trees.

account the retinue of the sub-Lord of the Manor consisted of fifteen, villeins with a household size of twelve, and bordars with six, produces a population total of 105 for the eleven households in Dilhorne in 1086.

	Lord of the Manor		Villeins	Bordars	Total
Dilhorne	Walter	15	60	30	105
Caverswall	Ernulf	15	120	12	147
Cheadle	Robert	15	91	6	112

Table 1. Population 1086

The higher number of villeins in Caverswall and Cheadle suggest that these communities were more prosperous than Dilhorne, and that in Dilhorne there would have been less of a social divide.

Footnotes

7. It may possibly be this Ulviet was the same individual who was the lord of post-Conquest Madeley as recorded in Domesday.

8. A carucate was approximately 30 acres. Churches were not normally listed as they were not taxable. This is the only mention of Stoke on Trent in the Domesday Book, and there is no other mention of the other half of the church, which lies in the Pirehill Hundred, rather than Totmonslow like Caverswall, Dilhorne and Cheadle. About 1155 Robert de Stafford (II) confirmed the grant of this half of the church to Stone Priory. SHC ii (I), p236.

9. Women rarely appeared in Domesday as they were far more restricted in how they could acquire land. It was rare that she could gain land as a result of service to an overlord or king. Godeva's holding of Cheadle may have been the result of her marriage settlement where a husband could provide for a widow after his death.

'Church End'

3. Manor and Landholding

Brief glimpses of manorial tenure and the more affluent individuals who lived in Dilhorne are seen through the abundance of assize rolls and plea rolls for Staffordshire. This period was before the advent of surnames where those mentioned carried the last name of de Dulverne to indicate where they were from. Less than forty years after the Domesday survey Radalphus de Dulverne was resident in 1120, followed by Ruald in 1166 and Robert sometime between 1185 and 1190.

The Manor transferred to the Bagot family of Bramshall in 1196 when Millicent, the sister and heiress of the last Robert de Stafford married Hervey.[10] He, like his predecessor, held the estate by service of a knight's fee[11] which was the common form of tenure for a Lord of the Manor holding an estate of the king. In return for the manor Bagot was obliged to provide military service to the king including arms, horses and men for up to a total of forty days active service each year. This was later converted to a money payment before finally being abandoned during the 17th century. Hervey Bagot probably remained on his own estate at Bramshall as a later Radalphus was also mentioned in 1199 and during the early part of the 13th century.

The first resident of Forsbrook was also recorded at the end of the 12th century when Osbert de Fotesbroc was in a dispute over land at Forsbrook with Radalphus.[12] About 1240 the township of Forsbrook, previously a dependency of Dilhorne, was merged with the Manor of Caverswall.[13] This did not alter the ecclesiastical jurisdiction or administration of Forsbrook which still remained within the parish of Dilhorne. Later the Manor of Dilhorne was held by Radalphus in his own right as part of a knight's fee.[14] He was still present in 1227[15] although two years later Robert was recorded as Lord of the Manor.[16] In 1243 Radalphus, possibly the third individual bearing this name, was recorded as being a knight.[17]

It may have been this Radalphus de Dulverne (now often shortened to the more conventional Ralph) who in 1254 was in dispute with William de Caverswall over the rights to a mill, mill-pond and thirty acres of land in Dilhorne along with a rent of 8s. The outcome was that William and his heirs were to hold the mill, the pond and the thirty acres for the annual rent of 2d. and with an admittance payment of 40s.[18] The Mill was again mentioned in 1297 when Ralph Freeman and his wife Elizabeth sued Margaret, the widow of Thomas de Rossynton for 5 messuages, $1^{1}/_{2}$ carucates of land, 8 acres of meadow and 4s of rent as well as a fourth part of a mill which they claimed to be the right of Elizabeth. As with the location of the original settlement, the location of this mill is difficult to determine. There are no substantial streams in Dilhorne, while Forsbrook, by virtue of its name, only possessed a brook. This does not mean that any one of these was impossible as they may have been diverted to a sluice to provide sufficient power. It may be possible that the mill was on the same site as the current mill at Blythe Bridge. Although within the parish this may have belonged to the manor of Forsbrook, which, as previously mentioned, had now been merged with the manor of Caverswall. It may have been this change that caused the discrepancy over who actually owned the mill, acting as a catalyst for the disputes.

By the beginning of the 14th century it is clear that the original manorial estate recorded in Domesday was being fragmented with portions now being held by different individuals.

Richard de Draycott's estates in 1305-6 included a freehold in Dilhorne held from Ronton Priory, his undertenant being Richard de Caverswall. This was confirmed again in 1311.[19] In 1332 William de Caverswall petitioned a request for a view of frankpledge and chattels called Waifs in his Manors of Caverswall and Dilhorne. This may have been an attempt by William to modify the system of tithingmen who were responsible for keeping the peace and dealing with anti-social behaviour. William proposed a reasonable fine and although an inquisition concluded that this would neither harm nor prejudice the King, the Chancellor refused to grant William the charter without the assent of King and Council.[20] This appeared to have been granted later the same year or the following year.[21] This division continued throughout the 15th and 16th centuries when in 1589 the Copwood family, then resident at Dilhorne Hall, were Lords of the Manor.[22] However, the manorial lordship did not descend with the Hall, passing instead to the Parker family of Park Hall, Weston Coyney, with whom it remained until into the 20th century.[23]

The following document records exactly the extent of the Manor at the beginning of the 19th century:

The Boundary of the Manor of Dilhorne as perambulated on Thursday the 25th day of September 1800 by the Jurymen and others of the Court held there on the day.

Commencing at the Gate on the Sweet Hill in the road to Draycott the boundary proceeds in a south-west direction down the side of the fence inclosed lands called Sweet Hills and continues along the fences of three fields called the Ox Closes keeping the Parish Boundary against Draycott into a meadow at the bottom of the Lower Ox Close where it turns nearly south along the east fence of the said meadow and of a piece of pasture land containing about seven acres to the south east corner thereof where the Boundary turns nearly west along the south fence of the field last mentioned into a piece of land called Bradshaws Quabbs[24] near Pittridge Pitts (which are in the adjoining land on the opposite or south side of the fence) so continues along the south fence of Bradshaws Quabbs to within about eighty yards of the south west corner of the same where the Boundary turns nearly south into Gallimores Quabbs and then proceeds to the south east corner thereof then turns and passes along the south fence of the quabbs last mentioned nearly in a west direction into a piece of land belonging to the poor of Caverswall called Stephen Stich[25] and so continues along the south fence of two other fields called Stephen Stich also belonging to the poor of Caverswall and a piece of land containing about two acres onto the Back Lane from Forsbrook to Draycott where the Boundary crosses the Lane through a Gate into a field called The Bottom and continues along the south fence thereof into the Uttoxeter Turnpike Road by the wooden stump where it crosses the turnpike into the further field in which are several pits and proceeds along the south fence of several fields called The Over Piece the [......] Bassy Leys, the Marl Field, and Toes Meadow to the River Blythe where it turns nearly in a northern direction along the course of the river through extreme corner of Tongue Sharp into the Churns Hole Meadow and from thence into the Perkins Meadow and the Long Meadow keeping along the west extremity thereof respectively (the Manor extending over all the said Meadows). From thence the Boundary continues by the side of the River Blythe into the Meadow head within about thirty yards of the north end thereof where it crosses Blythe Water between two willows into part of Blythe Marsh now called the further common field and continues along the south fence of some Inclosures other part of Blythe Marsh and then turns in a north direction by the side of the Gossy [?Brick Farm] along the west extremity of some Inclosures other part of Blythe Marsh into Stallington Lane which it crosses where a Gate formerly stood over a stile to another Inclosure also part of the Marsh and continues in a north east direction along the west side of two Inclosures other part of the Marsh Parallel with the foot road and continues by the west fence of a small

Inclosure to Blythe Bridge the Manor comprehending the whole of Blythe Marsh from thence the Boundary turns up Meer Lane to a Cottage in the occupation of Elizabeth Shenton then crosses the bottom or lower end of Queers meadow and the River Blythe in a north direction to the Mill Course crossing which it takes a west direction along the Mill Course to the end of the Queer Meadow at the Queer Gap then leaving the Mill Course in a north east direction by the side of the fence against land formerly of William Jolliffe esquire and now of the Honourable Booth Gray into a slang leading into Trowsy Lane which it crosses at a place where three lane ends meet and proceeds into a field called The Pringle on the east side of Brassington's Black Birches belonging to the Honourable Booth Gray and so passes by the side of the east fence of the Black Birches to a Stile on the foot way between Forsbrook and Caverswall Here the Boundary passes over the fence into Cash Heath Meadow and so along the Hedge between the Meadow and the Black Birches to a Gate in Cash Heath Lane then it turns in a north direction straight along the lane to the Carriage Way between Caverswall and Dilhorne and continues along the same Way to Cresswell Ford from then the Boundary proceeds up Stansmoor Lane to Tick Hill Gate and from thence passes up the middle of Tickhill end Bank direct for the corner of the Newlands along a foot path to a Gate and Meer Stone from thence down the lane to the entrance upon Caverswall Common and passing round the land allotted to Robert [?Rooke] esquire under the Dilhorne Inclosure Act in a straight line to another Meer Stone fixed upon the Common, close to a field belonging to Thomas Swinnerton esquire and so through the middle of the said field which is now in the occupation of Matthew Walter in a direct line to a Meer Stone near Blythe Hay Hedge from thence the Boundary turns eastward up the River Blythe head then by the north east side of land belonging to Thomas Swinnerton esquire in the occupation of the said Matthew Walter and taking in all the new Inclosed land at Wetley Moor it proceeds up the lane leading from Haywood Grange to a Meer Stone upon Wetley Moor called Whores Stone and so into the Turnpike Road leading from Cellar Head to Cheadle round the House and Lands of Richard Bolton and so directly along the Turnpike Road leading to Cheadle turning at the north east end of lands in the occupation of John Roby taking in all the lands in the occupation of the said John Roby From then the Boundary passes round Ellen Wright's Cottage and turns in a nearly south direction past the said Ellen Wright's down the ditch to Hewitts Lane from thence down the said Hewitts Lane by the course of a small brook into Dairy House Lane then proceeding along the course of Godley Brook to Birch Field Lane it crosses the said Lane with Godley Brook to Park Hall Farm House in the occupation of Joseph Woolescroft then continues down Godley Brook across Adderley Mill Lane following the course of the brook to the place where Boswells Brook enters into Godley Brook From thence the Boundary proceeds nearly west up Boswell Brook and leaving the brook passes by the north east side of Adderley Wood about seventy yards from the same and so in a straight line up a field called the Jane Riding to a stone at the south side thereof from thence it takes a south direction thro Weaneth Field to a Gate Place which [........] the Turnpike Road from Cheadle to Forsbrook where the Boundary crosses the Turnpike Road and proceeds in a straight line to a Meer Stone at the east end of Well Meadow and from thence to another Stone at the extremity of the south corner of Swines Croft and so turns directly westward to another Meer Stone on the south west side of Orchard Flatt and from thence westward in a straight direction to another Stone on the east side of Rough Field from thence to another Meer Stone in the same field The Boundary proceeds directly westward to Warrilow Field Lane and crossing the said lane continues through the middle of the outermost field belonging to Thomas Swinnerton esquire in a south west direction to the Gate at the top of Sweet Hill where the Boundary first began.

The survey is signed by: Joseph Chell, Thomas Heath, William Gallimore, Jeremiah Warner, Richard Gallimore, Joseph Chell junior, John Whalley, William Thorley, and George Parker, and shows that the manorial boundary was still coterminous with that of the parish boundary. The use of the word perambulation at the beginning of the document suggests that the boundary had been traversed. This ancient custom was more commonly associated with parish boundaries, when, usually at Easter, the vicar accompanied by his officers and other parishioners, would undertake to walk along the boundary of the parish, offering prayers at certain points.

Footnotes

10. Framed magazine article circa 1960s in the church.
11. Stafford Chartulary, Series II, no. XXV.
12. Assize Roll John 1, 1199. Osbert also appears four years later in the Assize Roll, John 5, 1203.
13. Framed magazine article circa 1960s in the church.
14. SHC, Vol.1880, p170.
15. Assize Roll 1227.
16. Plea Roll, Henry III, 1243, in SHC, Vol. IV, p76.
17. Plea Roll, Henry III, 1243, in SHC, Vol. IV, p96.
18. Calendar of Final Concords or Pedes Finium, Staffordshire, temp. Henry III in SHC Vol. IV, p244-245. Plea Rolls, Edward I, 26 Easter, (1297).
19. SHC, Vol.1925, p97. A document of 1332 records Peter de Shustoke granted land in Dilhorne to the prior and convent of Ronton [sic] Priory, Stafford. TNA C 143/215/12.
20. TNA. S 8/54/2689.
21. TNA, C 143/219/12. Inquisitions taken as a result of applications to the Crown for licences to alienate land.
22. Final Concords, Elizabeth I, 1582.
23. This is confirmed in a Court Survey dated 25th September 1800 with Robert Parker stated as being Lord of the Manor. Thirty years later this had passed to J H Parker of Park Hall (White's Directory of Staffordshire, 1834, p742), and by the 1860s had passed to Thomas Parker (Staffordshire Record Office D1343/6). By 1896 the Honourable Edward Swynfen Parker Jervis of Little Aston Hall, Stonnall was Lord of the Manor (Kelly's Directory 1896, p140). In 1904 William Robert Parker Jervis of Meaford Hall, Stone, was Lord, as well as in 1912 (Kelly's Directories of Staffordshire, 1904, p153, and 1912, p166). By 1928 Lt-col William Swynfen Whitehall Parker Jervis held the title, who with his wife Lady Fielden, were the chief landowners (Kelly's Directory 1928, p178). This was still the same in 1940 (Kellys Directories 1932, p174 and 1940 p171).
24. Quabbs means boggy ground.
25. A wall tablet in St Peter's Church at Caverswall records that 'John Browne, late of Caverswall, gent., and Ralph Browne, his father, late of the Meir and Cookshill, gent., left for the poor of this parish forever, 14 acres of land called the Stephen Stitches.'

4. The Merrie Community

The Subsidy Roll of 1327 was an attempt by Edward III to raise money to pay for a war against Scotland - yet another king following in both Alfred's and William's footsteps. Dilhorne contributed 16s. from seven men while Fotesbroc gave 24s. from ten. By comparison the Cheadle list contained twenty-six names, Caverswall twenty-three and Draycott fourteen. Compared with the population estimate based on Domesday (see Table 1) these figures suggest that Cheadle had now overtaken that of Caverswall, no doubt as a result of better communications and the right to hold a market, and that Dilhorne was still the least populated settlement.

Name (Dilhorne)	s.	d.
De Willo' fil' Symonis	ij	vj
Henr' del Delfe	ij	
Joh'e filio Willi	ij	
Ric'o Saundre	ij	vj
Henr' del Wal	iij	
Ric'o filio Willi	iij	
Rob'to de Stoundon		xij

Table 2. The Subsidy Roll of 1327 for Dilhorne

There is no way of knowing what proportion of the population these figures represent. From studies undertaken on other communities where contemporary tax lists exist alongside this 1327 assessment it is clear that the figures only correspond to about a quarter of the taxable population.[26] Taking this into account, and using a multiplier of six to represent household size, produces the following results. Although this figure may seem a little conservative it does produce a realistic estimate of the population, especially when compared to that obtained from Domesday.

	1086	1327
Dilhorne	105*	168
Forsbrook		240
Caverswall	147	552
Cheadle	112	624

Table 3. Population 1327

*The figures for Dilhorne and Forsbrook were not segregated in the Domesday Book. The combined figure for Dilhorne and Forsbrook here would give a population total of 408.

Life for these, and countless others, varied between subsistence and starvation, and England was far from merrie for the majority. The village had expanded during the 230 years since the Domesday survey although it would soon decrease by between one third and one half and would not reach a similar figure again until the beginning of the 17th century.

Roundel from nearby Checkley Church depicting reaping corn.

Roundel from nearby Checkley Church depicting mowing.

Roundel from nearby Checkley Church depicting hedging.

Of course not all of the inhabitants were peasants. During the 14th century a few managed to bargain for themselves farms of considerable size. The result of this was that even after paying manorial rents and church tithes they were able to make a profit.

The wooden houses, although differing in size, would have been similar in appearance to one another. The largest would have belonged to the prosperous gentlemen and yeomen (although these terms had yet to be applied), being up to 60ft by 25ft and consisting of three bays with an upper floor for sleeping, to the humble dwelling of the poor widow, probably no larger than 13ft by 13ft and containing just one room. The average family home, however, would have been approximately 40ft by 25ft.

All but the most modest dwellings were built on a stone plinth or foundation. These were constructed of two curved oak beams (crucks) secured to a horizontal ridge beam. The wooden frame would have been in-filled with cob walls painted white and illuminated with narrow windows. Roofed with thatch, this would have extended a good distance beyond the walls to protect against rain. For those who could not afford thatch, turf was used as a cheaper alternative. It was not unusual for most buildings to have a slightly warped appearance as the timbers, which were unseasoned, dried and hardened during their first few years. Most were built cheaply and quickly necessitating their rebuilding every thirty or forty years.

The toft, the area immediately surrounding the dwelling, had stones and pebbles stamped into the ground in an attempt to prevent a muddy morass in wet weather. A small fence ran around the toft and attached garden which was used to grow vegetables, fruit and herbs. Adjacent to the dwelling would have been any outbuildings - they may have included a brewhouse, bakehouse, stable, hen-house, and at a respectable distance, the privy or cess-pit. Possibly one or two individuals would have possessed the luxury of a beehive.

The interior of all houses, regardless of size, would have been dark. The small amount of light that came in through the window, and the doorway when the weather allowed it to be kept open, was augmented only by the light of tallow candles and the fire. This would have burned continuously, all day and all night, from late autumn through to spring. The bare earth floor would have been strewn with rushes.

Just as house size varied with status and wealth so too did furniture and possessions. The more prosperous would have had chairs, benches and chests, the latter acting as both a form of seating and a means of storage. The more humble dwellings with only one room would have had a trestle table, a bench and a couple of stools, and the sleeping area partitioned off with a wattle screen. Utensils would have included spits and gridirons for roasting, a cauldron for boiling, a few pans, and a bakestone. When not in use both utensils and tools would have hung from the beams or walls, and in winter, so too did joints of salted meat.

The most common form of dress during the 14th century for the majority of men was a tunic that reached down to the knees, usually russet red or blue, with a chaperon or hood, hose or chausses. Footwear consisted of calf-length boots or heavy felt shoes which in wet weather were protected by wooden clogs. Women would have worn a full-length tunic over a linen smock, as well as a linen wimple. However, not all were quite so fortunate. One such peasant appears in Piers Plowman's Creed:

> I saw a poor man by me on the plough hanging
> His coat was a clout that cary[27] was called
> His hood was full of holes and his hair cut
> With his knobbly shoes patched full thick

His tongue peeped out as he the earth trod
His hosen overhung his gaiters on every side
All beslobbered in mire as he the plough followed
Two mittens so scanty made all of patches
The fingers were worn and full of mud hung
This fellow wallowed in the muck almost to the ankle
Four heifers before him that weak had become
You could count all their ribs so wretched they were
His wife walked by him with a long goad
In a coat cut short, cut full high
Wrapped in a winnowing sheet to cover her from the weather
Barefoot on the bare ice that the blood followed
And at the field end lay a little bowl
And on it lay a little child wrapped in rags
And two of two years old on another side

This, no doubt, was the stark reality for many who toiled in the fields.

In the summer the roads were dry and dusty, and during winter usually wet quagmires which almost hindered rather than helped those who used them. The community would have appeared as one large farm. The cultivated land consisted of large fields divided into individual strips of approximately one acre. These were grouped into furlongs[28] and surrounded by baulks or paths to give access. It was in these furlongs that wheat, oats, barley or rye were grown. Every third one of these was left fallow in the traditional rotation farming method and grazed by cattle, sheep, pigs or goats. However these were not as large as modern-day animals as breeding programmes designed to increase size had yet to be introduced.

The large field behind the extension to the churchyard is bounded for the most part by a two-tier bank, with small ditches on either side, the corners of which are rounded rather than square. Although having the characteristics of a medieval deer park the enclosed area appears too small, however the demarcation does suggest an enclosure of some kind. If this was a deer park, albeit on a smaller scale, when in use the banks would have been more pronounced and the ditches deeper. The banks would have been topped with either an oak palisade or a fence, or a stone wall. Not all parks were of the conventional circular kind and the rectangular shape beneath St Thomas's Trees would have offered an ideal entrapment area when driving the deer downwards to leap over the boundary to be secured inside. Unfortunately no documentary evidence exists to support this.[29]

In addition to the cultivated land the Common would have provided grassland for sheep during summer, while low-lying meadows were used to grow hay. Fields were rarely bounded making it easy to stray from the road or footpath and for cattle to trample crops, a not unusual offence presented at the Manor Court.

It was at this Court that the operation of the Manor was administered. This was where the individual strips would be allocated to the peasants, stipulating that everybody grew the same crop in the same field and harvested at the same time, as well as regulations governing the labour required for the Lords own demesne land. Under the Lord of the Manor was the steward, and under him the bailiff, and finally the reeve, who was elected by the peasants as well as being one himself. It was he who saw to the smooth running of labour services and answerable directly to him was the Hayward with responsibility for hedges, the swineherd, the cowherd, the dairyman, and the foreman of the mowers.

Coarse bread was the staple diet of the 14th century, often eaten with cheese. Mutton and pork were still the main meats consumed, along with domestic fowls, hares, coneys (although this was technically poaching) and even wild birds. Another common meal was pottage, a type of lobby usually made with meat stock, chopped herbs, oats and salt, and often supplemented with peas and bacon pieces. Ale was the most popular drink, made from barley or oats but without hops, and sometimes flavoured with honey or herbs.

Like their Anglo-Saxon forefathers the majority of people did not venture beyond the limits of the village. Travel during this period was hazardous, especially long journeys when being robbed or even murdered was a reality. Also, particularly at the beginning of the 14th century, most peasants were still unfree and tied to the Lord of the Manor. When people did travel it was mainly for business, such as to the local market at Cheadle. This provided an opportunity for the exchange and sale of surplus goods. If a peasant had to pay a tax or a fine, either to the Lord of the Manor or the Church, selling at market was one of the ways of generating cash. Another reason for travel would be to one of the probate courts to prove a will. Fortunately these were peripatetic and included the neighbouring parish church of Caverswall. For those who had to travel to court at Lichfield the interior of the cathedral must have been a wondrous sight.

It was through travel that the folk of Dilhorne gained an awareness of what was happening in the wider world. At market travellers would have brought news of events elsewhere, as would the priest from the pulpit, and proclamations from the market place. Those in the quiet backwater of Dilhorne would not have been ignorant of who the King was, the outcome of wars, and disasters elsewhere.

Life was reliant upon the harvest. A three year span between 1315 and 1317 of excessively heavy rain resulted in cattle drowned in pastures and continual widespread crop failure. This led to starvation, often wiping out whole families or in extreme cases complete communities. If people did not die of starvation then death would occur from diseases connected with malnutrition. However, the worst was yet to come.

In 1348 and 1349 the plague known as the Black Death swept through England. The national population decreased by between one-third and one-half. With such a massive decrease in population houses stood empty, eventually decaying after being robbed of any useful building materials by the survivors. The once neatly farmed strips became overgrown and tangled with weeds as there was no longer a sufficient labour force to manage it. Faced with this shortage of labour some landowners had no alternative than to turn from arable to the less intensive livestock farming, and in particular sheep. From this point on it was far more profitable to sell wool than corn.

However, those that survived the Black Death found that for the first time they had the power to bargain. During the preceding century the change from providing labour services to the Lord of the Manor to a cash payment had slowly evolved. A peasant could also purchase his freedom by payment of a fine leaving him in a position to offer his services to the highest bidder. He was also free to travel in search of work, including if he wished, obtaining employment in one of the nearby towns.

Some attempt at redressing this shift of power resulted in the Statute of Labourers issued in 1349, which amongst other things, attempted to fix labourers wages.[30] A compromise was reached. Landowners who required labour services but were unable to attract workers began leasing land. This was for a set period, with a rent usually payable twice a year. At the end of the specified term the lease reverted back to the landowner. However, the same tenant was often able to begin a new term for the holding, and upon his death his offspring was able to accept tenancy on payment of an entry fine.

The list of seven names recorded on the Subsidy Roll of 1327 (see table 2) reveal that surnames were beginning to develop as evidenced from four of the individuals. The name Delfe, like that of Dilhorne, also originates from digging or delving, possibly indicating the occupation of Henry.

Before this period there was no need of surnames for the common folk. In Dilhorne an individual named Ralph was simply Ralph. If an individual had a popular name and needed to be distinguished from others in official documents, such as those generated by the Manor Court, they would be described as John of Dilhorne or John of Whitehurst, the 'of' being eventually dropped. However, these names were not hereditary at this point. It was only after the Black Death when people were more mobile that John Adderley, his offspring and their descendants, would also use this family name.

Although not being of any use to estimate population the Archdeaconry list of 1532 reveals the names of those who paid money into a guild to purchase prayers for their spiritual benefit. The list is arranged by parish with the most prominent members of the community, and presumably those who contributed the most, towards the top. What is immediately apparent between this and the subsidy roll of 1327 (see table 2) is the conventional use of surnames.

The entry for Dilhorne contains twelve families. However, by comparison to other places the entries for both Dilhorne and Draycott (with sixteen families) are short, although this is where the manuscript appears to peter out.[31] The standard entry consists of the name of the head of the family, the name of his wife (or wives in the case of remarriage), followed by any children.

Dilhorne   The Paroche of Delos the Sonday after Corpus Christe Day

Thomas Adderley, Joan, uxor eius, Thomas, John, Elizabeth, Humphrey, Joan, Margaret, Ralph, George, Alice, Dorothy.

Robert Warner, Ellen, uxor eius, Agnes, George, James, Henry, Edmund, Robert, Joan.

John Teylor, Ellen, uxor eius, John, Agnes, Richard, Joan, Margery, George, Joan, William.

William Heyne, Elizabeth, uxor eius, Thomas, John, George, Margery, Ellen.

Ralph Pyott, Elizabeth, Alice, uxores eius, Henry, Anna, Margaret, Joan, Ellen, Thomas, Alice, Richard, John.

Henry Philip, Margery uxor eius, Joan, John, Elizabeth, Robert.

Thomas Maburley, Alice, uxor eius.

John Warner, Ellen, uxor eius, William, Ralph, Christopher, Joan, Ralph, Margaret.

Christopher Wright, Alice, uxor eius, John.

James Amere, Joan, uxor eius, Margery, Thomas, John, Joan, Margaret, Ellen, Elizabeth, William, William, George, Roger, Joan, parentes.

John Warelow, Margaret, uxor eius, Emmot, Richard, Ralph, Agnes, Ellen, John, William, Ewen.

John Torner, Alice, uxor eius.

Below St Thomas's Trees. The earth embankment may possibly be the remains of the park pale.

Because this is a list of those wishing to be remembered in prayer, it is apparent (as with an examination of other parishes where contemporary information survives) that not all the names recorded may still have been living. This explains why Ralph Pyott gives the names of two wives, his first having died. Similarly, James Amere has two sons named William, one probably relating to an earlier child that had died. Amere also chose to include his parents who may also have been deceased. Taking into account these peculiarities the list suggests that the more wealthy of Dilhorne were now having large families with up to ten children.

Merrie England, if that's what it was, came to an abrupt end with the Reformation. This began in 1517 when Martin Luther, a German monk, began questioning what he considered to be the indulgences and abuses of his Catholic church. Others too, such as John Calvin, began publicly questioning the integrity of Catholicism. Little happened, however, until the Pope refused to grant Henry VIII a divorce from his first wife which led to England's break with Rome by the Act of Supremacy in 1534. Henry established himself as head of the new Protestant church, although this still included elements of Catholicism. The most ardent followers of this new religion were the Puritans. Until this point the majority of the interiors of churches, large and small, were emblazoned with colourful images of religious scenes covering the walls. The Puritans, considering this as a remnant of the old Catholic religion, obliterated these, usually by covering them with several layers of whitewash. Whether this occurred at Dilhorne is impossible to determine as any evidence was removed with the rebuilding in 1819.

Footnotes

26. W. G. Hoskins, 'The Population of an English Village 1086-1801. A Study of Wigston Magna' in 'Transactions of the Leicestershire Archaeological and Historical Society' Vol.33 (1957), p16.
27. Coarse cloth.
28. The term furlong here has no connection with the modern day unit of measurement, meaning a 'furrow-long' in length.
29. In the neighbouring parish of Cheadle are the areas known as Above Park and Little Above Park, both between Bank Top and the Cheadle to Cellarhead road. Dilhorne Park, where the Foxfield Railway Line currently terminates, appears to have been introduced by the railway.
30. It was this along with taxation for the French Wars that led to the peasant's revolt at the end of the century.
31. Leigh, for example, contains fifty-seven families, and Cheadle fifty-four, while Caverswall, Checkley and Croxden are omitted altogether.

The disused road running from Cash Heath to Cresswell Ford and incorporated as the route of both the parish and manorial boundaries.

5. The Church

The most unique feature of the parish church is the dominating octagonal tower, unusual for small churches. It is the only example in Staffordshire[32] although others exist at Hodnet in Shropshire and Hornby in Lancashire. It is possible that the tower existed before the church as a defensive structure. The abundance of round towers found in East Anglia built for this purpose were often incorporated into later churches. The fact that the tower has no doorway and only the smallest of windows at lower levels makes this theory more plausible. It is unlikely, although not impossible, that this may be a Saxon construction, possibly built by Goduin or one of the other thanes. However, if the tower was built as a defensive structure, it is more probable that this was erected by one of the first Normans who took the name of de Dulverne after the Conquest.

In all likelihood the first church at Dilhorne would have been a wooden construction. St Chad first brought Christianity to Britain in the 7th century, although it is impossible to say precisely when Dilhorne's spiritual needs were strong enough to warrant the building of a church. If the first church did predate the tower then this may have been attached to it or at least stood nearby.

The first mention of a church in documentary sources is 1166 when Ruald de Dulverne presented the advowson, the right to appoint the priest, to the Priory of Stone with the agreement of his overlord Robert de Stafford. This would have been a newly-constructed building of stone occupying the area of the current nave and incorporating the tower. By 1291 the church had been appropriated to the Dean and Chapter of Lichfield Cathedral.[33] The incumbent would have been given a house, glebe land which he would have farmed himself for his own sustenance, and the right to collect the tithes, a tenth of each of his parishioners stock. In return he was bound to keep the church in good repair[34], to financially assist those in need, and to provide hospitality to travellers.

The church was much more than simply a building to cater for spiritual needs. Being possibly the only stone building in the parish at this time it was also the meeting place for the community. Much of the business of the community would have been conducted in either the church, or as was more customary, the porch. It may even have been here where the Manor Court sat, and also used as a bank, being a place of deposit for any money or deeds that individuals felt uneasy about leaving in their less secure homes.

Following both the fashion in church building and the needs of a growing community the chancel was added in the 14thC.[35] This layout would have been unchanged until the addition of north and south aisles. Because both the nave and aisles were rebuilt in 1819 it is impossible to estimate when the originals were constructed although it is highly likely this occurred during the 15thC. The rebuilding of 1819 is most evident from the exterior, the large rectangular-cut stone blocks forming a marked contrast to that of the tower and chancel which flank them.[36]

A watercolour from the 18th century by an unknown artist shows the church from the south-west before the rebuilding of 1819.[37] The tower and chancel remain unaltered but the original nave and south aisle are clearly shown. The nave had three small rectangular clerestory windows of the Early English period, each incorporating a single vertical shaft. The height of the nave was lower than when rebuilt, being almost level with the height of the chancel. The south aisle, which had a steeper pitched roof than the current one, contained two large Early English windows. The one to the left of the doorway was round-headed with two vertical shafts

Dilhorne Church from the north.

Dilhorne Church from the north-east.

with Y-tracery. The one to the right was again divided by two vertical shafts but square-headed.[38] Both outside corners of the aisle were supported by two two-tier buttresses placed at 45 degrees matching those still existing at the corners of the chancel. The most obvious difference is the presence of the steeply-pitched south porch with the date of 1666 above the arched opening.

Externally the church is largely unadorned. On the east chancel wall are the remains of two renaissance tombs, one of which depicts a pair of cupids, minus their heads. At one time the heads were discovered and restored by the Rev G R Plant although again they have disappeared. On the north wall of the chancel can be seen the original priests doorway along with an Early English window, both blocked up. The square window of the south aisle may be from the original church based on a comparison with the 18th century watercolour. The two round-headed windows on the south aisle, and those on the north, were inserted during the rebuilding of 1819. However, an anomaly exists in another watercolour of the present church, also painted from the south-west.[39] This clearly shows a matching round-headed window replacing the square one. Why the artist decided to depict the church incorrectly is unknown.

A report on the fabric of the church in 1900 noted grooves caused by bowmen sharpening their arrows on the south side of the church.[40] These would have dated from 1543 when it was compulsory for men between the ages of sixteen and sixty in each town and village to practice archery after attending church on Sundays and Holidays. This practice continued until being abandoned during the 17th century.

The bells were first mentioned in the churchwardens' accounts of 1687 when Thomas Loton was paid 4s. for ironwork for the bells. It was during the 1680s, and into the first decade of the following century, that there were regular payments for ringing the curfew bell or ringing the 8 o'clock bell. The curfew had a dual function. It was rung at evening to warn villagers to extinguish their lights and fires as a precaution against accidental blazes, and secondly as a sign for taverns to close their doors. It also guided villagers home, as well as travellers to safety after dark or in extreme weather. The bells were also rung on special occasions such as Coronation Day and the Gunpowder Treason on November 5th, as well as to celebrate good news - including the Kings return in 1716. Further references include:

1692   For looking to the bells 2s.
1700   To a message for going to Newcastle to Thomas Swinnerton to take down the bells 6d.
1700   Paid Thomas Swinnerton of Newcastle for hanging the bells £4.
1703   To Thomas Loton for Ironwork 12s. 6d.
1763   Mending the bell clappers 8s.

The Lotons appear to have established themselves as the local blacksmiths and it may have been Thomas's son Richard who was paid 1s. 2d for mending the church lock and making a key in 1705.

By 1794 two of the four bells were described as 'crackd' and useless. At a vestry meeting it was decided to recast five tunable bells from the old metal. The expense for this undertaking was to be raised by subscription with any deficit met by levying an equal pound rate through the parish. A sixth bell was added in the 20th century by Foxfield Colliery in commemoration of those that died during the First World War. The clock on the exterior of the tower was installed by the Manningham Buller family in 1901.[41] This replaced an earlier one which had been in use since at least 1692 when John Fernihough was paid 8s. for tending the clock.

An interesting feature in the churchyard wall is the small Tudor-style doorway. This may have belonged to the school founded in the 16th century, although not in situ, as both illustrations and a parish map of 1839 position this immediately left of the main entrance gates. This doorway now gives access to a boiler house located directly beneath the tower. It was in the churchyard that a 13th or 14th century jug, probably made at Audlem, was discovered.[42]

The churchwardens' accounts reveal regular payments towards the upkeep of the church. These include repairs to the windows and the fitting of bars, and continual entries for replacing the bell ropes and fetching lime. Lime was used for whitewashing the walls of the church, either to obliterate any church paintings considered inappropriate in the 17th century, or as a way of brightening the interior. There were also payments for an unusual custom which appears to have been abandoned by the middle of the 18th century:

1692	paid Thomas Hollins for 4 bags of moss 11d.
1701	for moss and mossing the church 3s.
1703	for mossing and getting the moss 4s.
1730	for mossing the north side of the church 2s.
1733	Samuel Thorley churchwarden, myself, getting moss three days 2s.
1746	Moss for the church 7d.

The exact purpose of mossing the church is unclear although this may have been used to stuff under the eaves to absorb rainwater.[43]

The church naturally took a keen interest in its own resources, including what could be obtained from the churchyard. In 1800 one of the churchwardens', James Dunn, was reprimanded by the Rev. John Wolfe for 'mowing or cutting down docks, grass and other weeds growing [in the churchyard] and carrying the same away'. This was two years after the vestry had ordered that 'no cow, horse, mule, ass or hog shall be permitted to graze in the churchyard under pain or penalty of the owner being presented at the ecclesiastical court for such offence but that the clerk of the parish may be permitted to mow or cut such grass as may grow therein where no gravestone is and to take it off and to pay no rent for it'. Possibly Dunn had misunderstood the difference between clerk and churchwarden. However, three years later the vestry decided that James Dunn 'is not a sufficient and fit person to execute any parish trust or office and that in the future he be excluded from all such parish offices'. The following year the same vestry announced James Dunn 'is required to pay over the cash which he has collected for the use of the poor agreeable to the order of the magistrates or he will immediately be proceeded against for the recovery of the same. He is also required to produce all accounts respecting his churchwarden and overseership and payments to the said meeting that they may be instantly attained and laid before Mr Langford'. How Dunn's neighbours felt towards him is not known although he was certainly unpopular with the parish officers.

Although there is a stark contrast between the original stonework and the rebuilding of 1819 on the outside, internally there is virtually no evidence of rebuilding as the stonework flows harmoniously from tower to chancel. Some of the original stone appears to have been used for the internal walls. The arcades and clerestory are supported on four arches on either side, whose columns sit on octagonal bases. Six of the eight pillars display corbel heads, one of whom is Queen Victoria, who stares opposite at the Archbishop of Canterbury of the same period. The grooves found on the apex of the tower doorway were supposedly caused by bell ropes when the ringers used to stand towards the rear of the nave. The pattern of stonework behind the pulpit suggests that at one time there was a squint. Squints, or hagioscopes, to give them their correct name, enabled priests serving at altars at the end of the aisles, to synchronise with the priest serving at the main alter in the chancel. The north aisle may have been a chantry chapel, dedicated to a particular saint, although no record exists as to which one. No crusader tombs or effigies of the early de Dulvernes grace the interior. Their bones may still lie undisturbed beneath the churchyard soil. Those memorials that do exist commemorating the forefathers of the community are relatively modern which may be due to the rebuilding of the nave in 1819.

The floor is tiled throughout and a tile pavement for the parsonage was donated by the Minton factory in 1848, as well as those in the sanctuary three years later. These would have been installed during the rebuilding of 1819 or during the renovations of 1868. It was then that the plain wooden benches that now flank the central aisle were added to increase the seating capacity to 250. When the antiquarian William Pitt visited the church two years before the rebuilding of 1819 he noted the original box pews and the roof adorned with curious carved work.[44] Portions of the original pews can be seen incorporated as wainscoting in the chancel.

The plain, slightly oval font supposedly dates from either the Saxon or Norman period, although the circular base and octagonal shaft are modern. If this is correct then the font is the earliest of the furnishings within the church. The Jacobean altar table bears the date 1634 and the similarity of the altar rails would also suggest that these date from the same time. Both the pulpit and rood screen are relatively modern. The reredros was installed in 1906 in memory of John Beckett who had been vicar of Dilhorne for nineteen years.

Before the organ was installed in 1885[45] musical accompaniment was provided by the village orchestra. By modern-day standards the term orchestra was perhaps an exaggeration. Any parishioner who possessed an ability, to a greater or lesser degree, was enrolled to play instruments that often included a bassoon, hautboy (oboe), flageolet (flute), clarinet, and any other wind instrument available, along with the fiddle and violoncello.

If the altar is thought to represent the spiritual heart of the church then the parish chest may be compared as its administrative one. It was within this receptacle that the written documentation concerning parochial governance was once stored, including the parish registers which commence in 1561. The keeping of registers, recording baptisms, marriages and burials, was made law by a statute of 1538. The Act also included provision for securely storing these in a chest or other receptacle fitted with three locks so, in theory, the contents could only be accessed when the three keyholders, normally the incumbent and two churchwardens', were together. As with many examples, the chest at Dilhorne clearly predates the Act. Crudely constructed from oak, the hinged lid contains iron bands and also evident are the remains of what were the three padlocks used to secure its contents.

William Blake photographed both the exterior and interior of the church in 1921. Little has changed to the exterior with the exception of the removal of the parish notice board immediately left of the south door, and iron railings around a few of the graves, no doubt removed for the War Effort. Inside the church was lit by oil lamps suspended from the flat, white painted ceiling. The wainscoting that survives in the chancel also appears against the north aisle and west wall, broken only by the entrance to the tower. The year after Blake's visit a baptistry was completed. This was due to Sir William Thorley Loton of Perth, Australia, who had been born in Dilhorne in 1839, and who left a donation for this purpose.[46] He was the son of Joseph Loton, publican of the Hollybush. At the age of fourteen he departed for London and nine years later emigrated to Perth. He formed a mercantile business with interests in shipping, agriculture and pastoral developments. He became a director of a bank, building society and insurance firm, and later a Justice of the Peace. He served on both the education board and water board, was also a member of various agricultural societies, and had a successful political career spanning over twenty years. In 1923 he was made a knight bachelor. He died the following year at his house called Dilhorne and was buried at Karrakatta cemetery.

The priest's doorway and early English window (now both blocked up)
on the north side of the chancel.

Footnotes

32. This ignores the churches of St Mary's at Nantwich and Stafford as these towers begin above the central crossing.
33. Nichols, Isobel, in her introduction to 'The Monumental Inscriptions of All Saints Church, Dilhorne.'
34. Technically only the chancel, the upkeep of the nave fell on the parishioners.
35. Pevsner confirms the church as early 13th century in the lower parts and perpendicular above, with the chancel late medieval.
36. Nichols gives the precise date of 1402 for the building of the chancel.
37. Dilhorne Church, watercolour, anonymous, c1762-1802. William Salt Library, Stafford. SV-IV.15a (45/8039).
38. There may have been two windows to the right of the doorway which the projecting porch may be disguising.
39. Dilhorne Church, watercolour, anonymous [L. J. Wood], c1819-1899. William Salt Library, Stafford. SV-IV 15b. (45/8040).
40. Nichols. Obviously these would have been on either the tower or the chancel taking into account the rebuilding of the nave.
41. Nichols.
42. NSFCT, 1950, p83.
43. The churchwardens accounts for Askham in North Westmoreland contains an entry in 1738 for 'getting moss and mossing the church.' At Grasmere Church a custom existed of stuffing moss within the rigging to absorb the wet which ran from the ill-fitting slates. L. Armitt, 'The Church of Grasmere', Titus Wilson, Kendal (1912), p136. Charles Tiplady Pratt in a 'History of Cawthorne' suggests that the annual mossing of the church was a predecessor of rush-strewing to cover the floor (p160).
44. Pitt, William, 'Topographical History of Staffordshire', p231.
45. Kelly's Directory of Staffordshire, 1896, p140.
46. Kelly's Directory of Staffordshire, 1928, p178.

Dilhorne Church from the south.
Note the inclusion of iron railings around some of the graves which are now removed.

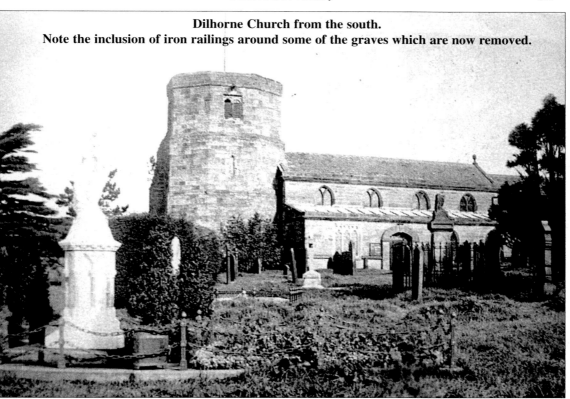

Dilhorne Church from the south.

The interior of the church looking towards the nave and chancel.

The interior of the church from the chancel looking towards the tower.

The bells.

The font.

The stone corbel depicting Queen Victoria.

The tiled sanctuary showing the communion table dated 1634.

The parish chest.

6. The Hall and other Major Buildings

It has been suggested that the first Hall at Dilhorne was built in 1270 and this was replaced by a second in 1377.[47] The first Hall would probably have been that occupied by Goduin before the Conquest. Goduin's successor, Walter, as Lord of the Manor may have chosen to erect a new building. This wooden barn-like structure would have been the largest building in the community, with possibly the exception of the church. The large interior, supported by vertical posts, housed just one room the focal point of which was the central hearth. One end may have been partitioned to provide a buttery and pantry, over which would have been the sleeping chambers of the family. Other household members would have slept in the main hall. During the 13th century this would have evolved into a two-storied house with the majority of the communal living area now being on the upper floor, with the service rooms below.

During the 1580s the Hall was in the occupation of the Copwood family[48] although by the end of the 1600s it had descended by the marriage of one of the co heiresses of the Copwood family to Philip Hollins.[49] Their son, Copwood Hollins, whose memorial is in the church, died without children in 1705, and bequeathed the property to his nephew Thomas Harrison. Despite being married three times both of Thomas Harrison's sons by his third wife Elizabeth died before reaching full age. His only daughter, Elizabeth, married John Holliday who then inherited the Hall. Holliday, a barrister at Lincolns Inn, erected a third Hall on the site, sometime before the end of the 18th century. The architect of this final incarnation was Thomas Trubshaw of Great Haywood.

This third Hall was a large Jacobean style three-storied house, the style of architecture reflected in the lodge which still survives with some modification. It was crowned with four large polygonal turrets and with the crest of arms of the Holliday family above the central portion.

Holiday was responsible for 'making the deep and almost impassible roads in the valleys delightful to travel over and of crowning the summits of the moorland hills with extensive and flourishing plantations'. The foundation of his improvements was laid in 1780 when a Bill in Parliament was obtained for 'dividing and enclosing the waste lands in the parish of Dilhorne and for making exchanges of lands from whence great scope of improvement and great convenience frequently spring'.[50] Holiday died in 1801 leaving the estate to his two-year-old grandson Edward Buller. His widow, together with his daughter Eliza, who married Sir Francise Buller Yarde Buller, baronet of Lupton in Devon, managed the estate until his grandson came of age.[51]

Edward (later Sir Edward) Buller's first wife was Mary Ann, the daughter of Major General Coote Manningham and sister and heir of Boyd Pollen Manningham. From this point the family adopted the double-barrel name of Manningham-Buller. Mary Ann died in 1860 and three years later Sir Edward married Georgina Charlotte, daughter and heiress of Sir Charles Edmund Nugent, and widow of George Banks, MP. Sir Edward's eldest son, Morton Edward Manningham Buller, born 1825, succeeded as second Baronet on the death of his father in 1882 and remained at Dilhorne Hall. He became the largest landowner of the parish with about 90% of the houses and farms, although was never Lord of the Manor. Sir Morton married Mary, the eldest daughter of William Davenport of Maer Hall in 1863, while two of his brothers, Reginald and Frederick, also married daughters of William Davenport. Sir Morton became Lieutenant-

The front and north side of Dilhorne Hall.
Photo courtesy of Aubrey Salt.

The front of Dilhorne Hall.

Colonel of the 3rd Battalion North Staffordshire Regiment, and Hon. Colonel from 1888. He also became a JP and acted as Deputy-Lieutenant for Staffordshire[52] until his death in 1910. His widow, Lady Mary, left for Sutton Rock near Chesterfield although she returned to Dilhorne on numerous occasions before her own death in 1923.

It appears that all of Sir Edward's sons were attracted to military life. His second son Edmund (1828-1897) joined the Rifle Brigade at the age of seventeen and served through the Kaffir Wars of 1846 and 1852. He commanded the 1st Battalion between 1871 and 1876 and became Major General. He married Lady Ann, the daughter of Thomas, the 2nd Earl of Leicester, at the age of forty-six in 1874. Sir Edward's third son, Coote (1829-1868), also served alongside his brother Edward in both Kaffir Wars. He took part in the Crimean Campaign and was also present at the battles of Alma and Inkerman, but was severely wounded at the Siege of Sebastopol. Sir Edward's fourth son, Reginald (1831-1888), served in the Coldstream Guards in the Egyptian Campaign of 1882 and was also present at the Battle of Tel-el Kebir. Sir Edward's youngest son Ernest (1839-1888) commanded the Second Battalion of the Rifle Brigade and served on the staff of the Zulu Campaign in 1879, the Boer War of 1881, and was present at the battles of Ginghilouo and Ulandi.

Sir Edward's eldest son and successor Sir Morton had three daughters, one of whom, Evelyn, married Major Sir William Henry Fielden of Doveridge and Feniscowles and so the Hall passed to this family who were resident during the first part of the 20th century.[53] Their son, William Morton Buller Fielden, was known as Master Billy throughout the community. He had taken a practical course in estate management at Gainsborough with the intention of farming the estate. In May 1914 William celebrated his 21st birthday at the Hall. The village was decorated with evergreen arches, bunting and flags, and the whole community was treated to a tea at the school, while the farm tenants enjoyed an evening supper at the Royal Oak.

In 1923 the Hall was finally vacated by the Fieldens who moved to Doveridge. The Hall was offered for sale although failed to attract interest. The sale catalogue describes the large panelled drawing room, dining hall, library, living rooms, twenty bedrooms with dressing rooms, bathrooms, ten servants rooms, extensive kitchens and stable block and coach house. Because the Hall failed to sell it was demolished in 1927 and the surrounding woodland cleared, including that covering Callowhill and St Thomas's Trees, to reveal a stark hillside.

Although the Fieldens left Dilhorne they remained influential in the area and continued supporting the church. They still possessed 538 acres of land and woods along with some of the best properties including Home Farm, Hall Farm, Stansmoor Hall, Holly Bush House, Church House, the old Grammar schoolhouses, and numerous cottages that were not sold until 1943.

The site of the Hall became the Miner's Welfare Institute opened by Sir Felix Brunner in 1934. This was financed by Foxfield Colliery with a levy deducted from employees wages for the privilege of using it. This was inherited by the parish council when the colliery closed and in 1969 the Institute became the Dilhorne Recreation Centre. The foundation of the main Hall was made into a crown bowling green and tennis courts and the rose garden became the site of the third vicarage built in the 1930s. It was here that a garden party was held in 1959 opened by Sir Reginald Manningham Buller who was Attorney General, Lord Chancellor, and later in 1966 the first Viscount Lord Dilhorne. At the event he was joined by the Fielden family of Doveridge and spoke of his fond childhood memories of the Hall. This was the last time a member of the Manningham Buller family was to visit the community. Sir William Buller Fielden, the last of his line, died in 1976 and the barony passed to his cousin. The entrance to the site still survives although it has been altered slightly and moved to the left of the lodge. The original entrance ran through what is now the centre of the lodge which was of a gatehouse design.

A watercolour shows the Hall before being rebuilt by John Holliday during the 18th century.[54] This was a three-storey building with a slightly projected central pediment, with a span of five windows across the first and second floors. Attached to the left side of the main block appear two three-storey bays. The architectural style suggests that this had been built towards the end of the 17th century. Also visible on the same painting is the church, the house at St. Thomas's Trees, the old parsonage and the windmill.

The windmill was situated on the Common to the left of the road from Dilhorne to Boundary immediately after the road finishes its climb from the Royal Oak. How long this had been in existence, or had occupied this naturally windy spot, is impossible to determine. By the 18th century this probably incorporated a head that appeared to be an upturned wooden boat at the top of the tower. This part was not fixed but instead sat on the rim of the tower and was designed so that the position of the main sails could be changed to take advantage of different wind directions. This was accomplished by a small circular vane at the rear of the head. When the wind changed direction and the main sails stopped rotating the wind would operate the vane which would then turn the sails to face the wind again, which in turn would cause the vane to stop. This meant that the sails would automatically always face the wind.

By the middle of the 19th century the mill was tenanted and worked by Silas Jackson. He had been born in Caverswall in 1806 and had married Mary Ann from Dilhorne. They had two children, both born in Dilhorne, Anna in 1849 and Samuel born in 1852. During this time Silas, who was recorded as a miller and shopkeeper, was also employing two teenage servants. By the early 1870s Samuel also helped his father with the mill. Ten years later at the beginning of the 1880s, and now aged seventy-five, Silas had retired with Samuel taking over from his father as miller. The mill must have ceased operating during the 1880s, for in 1891 Samuel was miller at the Mill House at Kingstone near Uttoxeter.

Other principal buildings within the parish include Blake Hall. This was first mentioned in 1299 when Felicia, the widow of William Blakehalgh, sued Henry, son of William de Blakehalgh for a third of a messuage and thirty acres of land in Dilhorne for her dowery. At the trial Henry failed to appear and the sheriff was requested to summon him and to take the dowery claimed into the Kings hands.[55] By the 15th century Blake Hall had become the home of the Adderley family until the 18th century. The estate then passed to the Colcloughs, the Swinnertons, and later the Pilkingtons.[56]

The Whitehursts were first mentioned in 1309 when Almarcia, the widow of Hugh le Heywood of Dilhorne was disputing ownership of eight acres of land at Dilhorne against William de Whytehurst, as well as eight acres of land against William's son Thomas.[57] Slightly later William, the son of William de Whitehurst, sued his brother Richard over a messuage, seven acres of land and two acres of meadow.[58]

Heywood Grange is a large stone-built house which dates from 1672.[59] This two-storey dwelling consists of a hall and cross-wing (to the left) with a two-storey porch to the front.

Stansmoor Hall is a large stone-built house of two stories and dates from the mid-17th century.[60] Each of the three gables at the front and rear contain mullioned windows, as do the attics, giving the appearance that the building is of three storeys.

Almost adjacent the church is Church House. The name occasionally appears in parish records of other communities as being the forerunner of the parish hall. Before the Reformation this was where church ales were brewed and served - a popular method of raising money for the church. (At Elvaston and Ockbrook in Derbyshire four ales were brewed throughout the year). During the 20th century the hall was used by the Ladies Fellowship, and by the 1960s the youth club.

Malt House Farm, although rebuilt in brick during the early 19th century, is of the long house design which reveals something of the building that would once have occupied the site. This would have been a medieval farmhouse where the household occupied one half of the property, with accommodation for livestock in the other. The name derives from beer being brewed in the barn section of the house during the 19th and early 20th centuries.

The pair of large semi-detached houses on New Road opposite the church also contain earlier stonework around the base.

Many of the buildings in the community have the pretensions of being brick-built 18th century town houses, much larger than expected for such a small rural community.[61] These may have been built on the profits of coal as the wealth of the community rapidly increased during this period.

Footnotes

47. Short, George W., p14. How these precise dates have been arrived at is uncertain, especially in the absence of any documentary evidence.
48. Final Concords, Elizabeth I, 1582.
49. Account of the Parish of Dilhorne sent to Stebbing Shaw, 1797. William Salt Library MI48.
50. Account of the Parish of Dilhorne sent to Stebbing Shaw, 1797. William Salt Library MI48.
51. Walton, Cathryn and Porter, Lindsey, 'Lost Houses of North Staffordshire' Landmark Collectors Library, 2006, p65. His grandson was John Buller Yarde Buller. An alternative account claims that the third version of the Hall was built in 1837 by Edward Buller.
52. Court Guide and County Blue Book of Warwickshire, Worcestershire and Staffordshire, 1902.,p336.
53. Kelly's Directory of Staffordshire 1912, states Dilhorne Hall as being the seat of Mrs William Henry Fielden (p166).
54. Dilhorne Hall, watercolour, anonymous [Stebbing Shaw], c1762-1802. William Salt Library. SV-IV.14 (45/8013).
55. Plea Rolls, Edward I, 1299.
56. Framed magazine article circa 1960s within the church.
57. Plea Rolls of Edward II, Hillary 3, 1309. The variations of spellings are reflected in the original documents.
58. Plea Rolls, Edward III, 1327-1377.
59. Pevsnser. The Tudor arch lintel is inscribed 'IS 1672.'
60. Pevsnser.
61. Particular examples are numbers 11 and 14 on the High Street.

The tennis courts at the Welfare Institute, to the left; the bowling green seen in front.
Photo courtesy of Aubrey Salt.

The Miners Welfare Centre before the building was dedicated to the village as a Recreation Centre. (1963).

The Welfare Institute built after the demolition of the Hall.
Photo courtesy of Mick Faulkner.

The Welfare Institute built after the demolition of the Hall.
Photo courtesy of Aubrey Salt.

The site of the windmill on Dilhorne Common (known locally as the 'Rocks').

The gatehouse to Dilhorne Hall showing the original entrance.
Photo courtesy of Mick Faulkner.

The south front of Dilhorne Hall, showing the drive up from the gatehouse and the porch.
Photo courtesy of Mick Faulkner.

The front of Dilhorne Hall.

Note the 2-man power mower.

Photo courtesy of Mick Faulkner.

Old Church House.

Church House, immediately north of the churchyard, the other side of the road to Old Church House.

Malthouse Farm. The layout is possibly of the medieval longhouse design with the household accommodated in one side and livestock in the other.

Dwellings on New Road opposite the church. Incorporated into the base is stonework from a previous dwelling on the site

7. Population and Housing during the 17th Century

Before the 10 yearly census began at the start of the 19th century it is difficult to be precise about population statistics. Only sporadic lists exist, one of which is the Hearth Tax of 1666. This was first introduced in 1662 by Central Government, the rationale being that hearths were fixed and easily identifiable, unlike individuals who could evade the assessors. Its unpopularity suggested its efficiency and in less than thirty years it was abolished. This list not only provides information for a population estimate but also the distribution of wealth. It should be noted that the number of hearths does not indicate the number of rooms in a property as some would have been unheated. If houses were exempt it did not mean that they did not possess a hearth, but households that were free from the payment of church rates, either because they occupied property worth less than 20s. annually or as owners of premises worth less than £10.

Samuel Adderley formerly Ralph [of Blake Hall]	6	Ralph Whewall	1
Mr Edward Doughty	8	John Jenkinson	1
Joseph Lees	5	Richard Turnock	1
William Mountford	1	Thomas James and his tenant	3
John Fenton	1	John Dickes	2
Edward Tayler	1	John Wood	2
Richard Whitehurst (of Whitehurst)	4	John Hurst	1
Mr Thomas Pyott	3	Thomas Salt	1
Thomas Hasloms tenant	2	Mr Thomas Dresser [d.1670]	2
Thomas Whitehurst	2	Thomas Bull	1
John Worribe	1	Robert Bullocke	1
Thomas Bentiley	1	John Smith	1
Adam Colclough gentleman (of the Delph House)	5	Richard Johnson	1
Thomas Collier	2	Thomas Shaw	1
Mr Thomas Homes	1	William Hollins	1
John Harvey	1	Thomas Loton	1
Raph Tayler	1	Francis Harvey	1
Robert Martin	1	Widow Smyth	1
John Paikeman	1	Widdowe Bull	1

Table 4. Hearth Tax Dilhorne Township (Occupiers and number of hearths)

For the assessment Dilhorne was included in the Caverswall constablewick[62] This was divided into six townships, four in the parish of Caverswall and two in the parish of Dilhorne. The four within the former were Caverswall itself (including Cookshill), Weston Coyney, and the 'hamlets' of Meir and Hulme. The two in the latter were Dilhorne itself and Forsbrook. Smaller hamlets in both parishes were ignored, no doubt the individuals being listed where the compiler thought most appropriate. The list shows the expansion of surnames although of the thirty-eight individuals only three shared the same name Bull, Tayler and Whitehurst.

The forty-seven exemptions were listed together at the end of the list rather than in their individual townships. Because of this they were proportionally divided[63] to estimate the total number of dwellings in each township. This figure was then multiplied by the average household size (4.1) to estimate the total population for each township.[64] 30% of the households in the constablewick were exempt from payment compared with the lower figure of the national average,[65] suggesting that, as a whole, the parish was reasonably wealthy.

TOWNSHIP	HEADS TAXED	EXEMPTIONS (ACTUAL 47)	TOTAL HOUSEHOLDS	TOTAL POPULATION
Dilhorne	38	11.5	49.5	202.9
Forsbrook	39	12	51	209.1
Careswall	28	8.5	36.5	149.6
Weston Coyney	29	8	38	155.8
Meare Hamlet	6	2	8	32.8
Hulme Hamlet	15	4.5	19.5	79.9
Total	155	46.5	202.5	830.1

Table 5. Proportional division of the population within the constablewick.

Comparing this population estimate with the former two reveals that Dilhorne was now considerably larger than Caverswall.

TOWNSHIP	1	2	3	4	5	6	7	8	10	20	TOTAL
Dilhorne	25	6	2	1	2	1		1			38
Forsbrook	30	5		3		1					39
Careswall	14	4	4		5					1	28
Weston Coyney	22	3			1		1		2		29
Meare Hamlet	3	2		1							6
Hulme Hamlet	6	4	3	1	1						15
Total	100	24	9	6	9	2	1	1	2	1	155

Table 6. Distribution of hearths within the constablewick.[66]

The majority of people appeared to live in humble one-hearth dwellings. Although Dilhorne and Forsbrook have almost identical figures there appeared a higher ratio of poorer housing in the latter. The same also occurred for Caverswall and Weston Coyney respectively. By comparison the Cheadle list contained 122 people taxed with eighty-four exemptions, giving a combined total of 206 and using the same methodology produced a population total of 844.

Contemporary with the Hearth Tax was the Compton Census of 1676. This was a single census undertaken by Henry Compton, the Bishop of London, in an attempt to determine religious adherence. The census supposedly recorded all those over the age of sixteen, which has been estimated as applying to between 60% and 70% of the population. The census recorded that the parish of Dilhorne, inclusive of Forsbrook and the small settlement at Blythe Marsh, contained 351 conformists, eleven non-conformists and two papists. Taking this combined total of 364 and adding 120 to include all those under the age of sixteen produces a population estimate of 484. Considering that this figure contains Forsbrook and Blythe Marsh the estimate appears fairly reliable when compared to that produced from the Hearth Tax.

The interiors of some of the houses in Dilhorne during this time may be glimpsed from the probate inventories that survive. It must be remembered that these were simply lists of what a person had at the time of their death. Many items may already have been disposed of, and those who were aged may have been living with children or other family members and therefore owned relatively little. They were compiled by appraisers, who were often neighbours or relatives of the deceased, one of whom would have had sufficient knowledge to accurately value the contents. The way appraisers worked differed widely, varying from the simplistic total valuations of goods of a certain kind anonymously combined together, to the extremely detailed listing all possessions and compiled on a room by room basis.

Individuals were usually described by their status, rather than their occupation, although the term husbandman could be taken as both. From a selection of twelve inventories between 1660 and 18 there were three gentlemen, three husbandmen, two yeomen, a miner, a clerk, and two where status or occupation was omitted. The difference between gentlemen and yeomen was that while a gentleman may have acquired his income from various sources, the yeoman's income was derived exclusively from agriculture. Husbandmen, like yeomen, also relied upon agriculture but generally occupied smaller farms.

The most popular form of seating was chairs, followed by stools and forms, the latter usually flanking long tables. Two of the inventories neglect to mention any form of seating, although both of these contain coffers which were also used as seats, with additional comfort provided by cushions. Cupboards were a common form of furniture. These were usually side tables, often with a series of shelves for displaying silver, pewter or earthenware. Less common were the two individuals with presses in which clothes or household linens were stored. The most popular storage items were coffers, followed by chests and boxes, often used for storing clothes and linen.

Items of brass and pewter were often valued as simple totals rather than being listed individually, thereby disguising many individual items. For those items of pewter that were listed the largest number were dishes and spoons, followed by flagons, candlesticks, porringers, salts and chamber pots. Brass was more common with kettles, pots, pans and skillets being the most numerous. But it was iron that was by far the most common metal of household utensils, largely due to the implements associated with the fire and cooking. Like brass and pewter, not all items were listed individually, and phrases such as 'iron things in the chimney' were not unusual. The most common items were pot-hooks and racks, fire shovels, tongs, backstones, spits and grates. Other utensils included pots, kettles, dripping pans, jacks, toasting irons, frying pans, creepers, andirons, slices, brunderts and cobberts.

These items throw light upon the cooking practices of the period. Meat was roasted on a spit in the fireplace. Pot-hooks hung from the chimney for suspending pots over the fire for boiling, an alternative method being pot-racks. Baking was accomplished on a large flat stone or iron plate commonly called a backstone, an alternative method being bread ovens built into the chimney. However, because these were regarded as a fixture they went unrecorded.

Household objects of wood were often grouped together disguising individual items. The majority appears to have been used for brewing, dairying and storage, along with washing and salting. Those items that were specified included barrels, tubs, churns, looms and books. These last two both have double meanings and rarely did appraisers make any distinction. In the two inventories in which looms appeared they were listed alongside other wooden wares and therefore were taken to mean a large open tub or vat rather than a machine for weaving. Similarly the books that appeared were also found among wooden ware and taken to mean a pail or bucket.

All but one of the twelve inventories made some form of reference to husbandry ware. Nine stated 'all his husbandry ware' or a similar phrase thereby disguising individual items. Ploughs were mentioned in five inventories, harrows and wains in four, and carts in three. Other items that were individually mentioned included shovels, pitchforks and mattocks.

Livestock was mentioned in all the inventories. This ranged from Richard Colclough with only ten sheep through to those with large quantities of various cattle. With the exception of Colclough all of the other individuals possessed cows, a total of 127 including twenty-four twinters (a beast of two winters old), five heifers and forty-seven calves. Those with both cows and calves were probably engaged in stock rearing. Only three people possessed a bull and three had bullocks. Nine inventories listed a total of thirty-nine stearks, young bullocks or heifers between one and two years old. The three individuals who possessed bulls also had oxen, with quantities of six, five and four, the latter of whom also had four stears, young castrated oxens. A total of fourteen horses were found among seven inventories. With the exception of the five stated as cart horses it was impossible to determine whether these were for riding or draught animals because saddles were rarely mentioned, being disguised under the often used 'all husbandry ware' phrase.

Sheep were the most numerous form of livestock. These cost very little to maintain, provided wool, and cheese could be made from their milk. A total of 288 were found among nine individuals. James Cresswell owned the largest flock with eighty-three down to John Buxton with just two. Eight individuals were recorded with swine, possessing between one and three. Pigs were regarded as one of the stand-bys of the lower classes. Only those with enough kitchen waste would have kept pigs, although those engaged in dairying would also have fed them on whey. Only four individuals possessed poultry, including one with geese, although no further descriptions or quantities, other than in monetary values, were stated.

The most numerous crop was corn, found in six inventories. Only one of these stated corn upon the ground meaning growing, the other five often being mentioned as in the barn or in the house. The majority of corn was probably wheat, although this was only mentioned once by name. Adam Colclough also possessed quantities of harvested barley and oats. Six people possessed hay, and four had manure, a valuable commodity before the advent of artificial fertilisers.

All twelve individuals were assigned a value for ready money. This was always combined with clothing under the term purse and apparel. This averaged between £1 to £3 for each person, and ranging from 10s. up to £10, although this amount also included a watch and a ring. Richard Colclough's inventory was the only one to list individual items of clothing, not only his own but also those of his deceased wife. His consisted of two shirts, two pairs of breeches, two coats and two hats. What remained of his wife's clothing consisted of a gown, two petticoats, two aprons and a flaxen smock. These were stored in two coffers with a total value of £1. Besides money there were also two references to credit. Thomas James had bills and bonds worth £25, while Robert Sale had £3 of unspecified debts owing to him.

Debts are more often recorded in wills. That of Elizabeth Salt, dated February 13th 1625 contains a number of debts owing to her late husband and still unpaid. These she bequeathed to her son:

Item I give to the above said Raphe Salt these debts as followeth. First of Raphe Brown £3 8s. 4d.

which is owing for shoes; which William Danbury oweth for Clarke's wages; the money which Thomas Daleman ought my husband for shoes which cometh to 5s.; the money which Richard Hammersley ought my husband for shoes which cometh to 4s.; the money which William [ileg.] ought to my husband for shoes which cometh to 2s. 2d.; the money which Mr Colclough ought my husband for tending the bells 10d.

This last entry is also the first reference to the church bells, preceding any mention in the churchwardens' accounts. Her will also states 'my best beast for my landlord' indicating that the custom of heriot was still enforced by the manor.

Appraisers ignored food that was for daily consumption, only listing processed or stored food such as butter, cheese, beef and bacon. Six inventories contained reference to some form of provisions, the most numerous being cheese. This, unlike butter, needed time to mature therefore increasing its chances of appearing in an inventory. Four made reference to bacon, and two listed both butter and beef. The inventory of Ralph Hollins mentioned 'one cheese presse one churne with all & singuler Barrells'. The appraisers of Adam Colclough discovered 'In the store chamber about two hundred of cheese along with six cheese boards and other provisions'. Robert Sale possessed twenty-nine cheeses in addition to 'In the cheese chamber sevenscore & 15 cheeses'. These individuals probably produced for the Uttoxeter market, already established for its dairy produce.

Ten of the twelve inventories mentioned the names of rooms within the house. It is important to understand that an inventory would not necessarily list every room of a building. Appraisers were not concerned with the layout, only the goods within. Furthermore there would be no need to count empty rooms, or those occupied by others if the deceased had been living with kin. Also these inventories represent only a slight fraction of the wealthier individuals of the parish. Many of the other dwellings would have been far less luxurious. The commonest type of farmhouse had only four rooms: a hall or houseplace, a parlour bedroom, a service room, and one chamber on the first floor primarily for storage, but in the case of large families, doubled as extra sleeping space. For the less fortunate the smaller two-roomed single-storied dwelling would have been home, the cruck method of construction still common until the 17th century. A storage loft may have existed over one of the rooms, accessed by a ladder.

If an upper chamber was used exclusively for storage it was sometimes more convenient not to fasten either the joists or the floorboards so that they could be moved to get bulky items into the chamber. Therefore they may appear valued in inventories, showing that they were regarded as moveable goods, as in the inventory of James Cresswell which mentioned boards over the stable.

Common to all dwellings was the central hall or houseplace, flanked with parlours, chambers, or both. By the 16th century the conventional single hall had evolved with the introduction of these parlours and chambers on the ground floor emphasising the need for a family's seclusion and privacy. The most numerous service room was the buttery, found in six of the ten dwellings, compared to only four that mentioned kitchens. Butteries were normally found on the north or north-west side of the building for the sake of coolness, lighted by a slatted window and furnished with numerous shelves and benches.

The smallest dwellings were those with only four rooms occupied by miner Ralph Hollins and husbandman Robert Hill. The houseplace of Ralph Hollins was the main room for both cooking and eating. This was furnished with a long table flanked with two forms. His brass and pewter were displayed on a cupboard and around the fire lay the necessary ironware for cooking. The parlour had the dual purpose of both entertaining and sleeping which was not uncommon during the 17th century. Besides what appeared to be the principal feather bed complete with curtains and valance was a table, a form and stool. The upper chambers, over both the houseplace and parlour, were bedrooms and storage areas. Both his cheese-making and brewing equipment were likely to have been in the barn which was also used to store his barley, hay and straw.

A true Inventory of all & singular the goodes Cattle and Chattells of Ralph Hollins late of the parish of Dilhorne also Dilverne in the County of Stafford myner deceased taken the sixteenth day of ffebruary in the three and thirtieth yeare of the raigne of our Soveraigne Lord Kinge Charles the second And in the yeare of our Lord God 10 as foloweth:

		£ s d
Imprimis	Twoe cowes and three twinter heafors	9-0-0
Item	one ould mare	0-10-0
Item	two little swine	0-10-0
Item	The hay in the barne with a little barley and a little strawe	1-0-0
Item	ffive peeces of squard timber lyinge in the lane over against the house	0-6-0
Item	In the Dwellinge House place one long table with a fframe and twoe fformes	0-6-8
Item	One seild Cupboard	0-5-0
Item	Twelve pewter dishes ffoure pewter flagons one pewter chamber pott twoe pewter porringers one pewter candle sticke twoe pewter Salts & some spoones	0-6-8
Item	ffowre little brasse kettles Twoe Skelletts one brasse pott three iron potts one warmeinge pan	0-17-0
Item	One Iron dreepinge pann Two Grates with Creepers, Two paire of pott racks one paire of Tonges one fire shovell one tostinge Iron one ffryinge pann one Beefe forke, one Rostinge hooke one paire of Bellowes, one Gun & one smoothinge Iron	0-8-0
Item	one Salt Coffer, one Dish Crate	0-1-0
Item	In the parlour one Table with a fframe one joyned fforme one joyned stoole	0-4-0
Item	one paire of seild Bedstocks with a ffeather Bedd Bolsters Coveringe & Blanketts with Curtens & vallens	1-2-6
Item	In the chamber over the house one paire of seild Bedstocks one feather Bedd one feather Bolster one Coveringe and twoe Blanketts	0-18-0
Item	one Table with a fframe	0-4-0
Item	Three Coffers and twoe Truncks	0-10-0
Item	one Kymnell	0-3-0
Item	hempe Drest & undrest	0-3-0
Item	In the chamber over the parlour three paire of Bedstocks, one ffeather Bedd, one chaffe bed with bolsters Coveringes blanketts Curtains & Vallens	1-0-0
Item	one Chest one Coffer	0-6-0
Item	all the napery ware	0-13-4
Item	one cheese presse one churne with all & singuler Barrells brewinge Loomes tubs Bowkes peales Benches shelves tressells wheeles chayres stooles dishes packsadles pannyers husbandry ware and all other goodes thinges & comodities which seen herein before not praysed	0-13-4
Item	money in his purse and his weareinge apparel	0-10-0
	Sum total	19-18-02

Praised by us whose names are hereunto subscribed the day & yeare aforesaid
Edward Titterton   the marke T of Thomas Dickes   John Dix

The inventory of Robert Hill of Blakeley Bank was far more simplistic. His four rooms consisted of a houseplace, house chamber, parlour and parlour chamber. His houseplace contained a table and cupboard on which was displayed his brass and pewter. The house chamber contained three coarse beds and a coffer. The parlour had a bed of greater value along with a coffer, and his parlour chamber a further bed and some provisions. Perhaps the bareness of his home is demonstrated by the fact that his livestock and agricultural implements were valued at three times more than the house with all its contents.

Richard Colcloughs appraisers listed only three rooms, a parlour, a chamber and a buttery, although from the methodology of his appraisers it is apparent that a houseplace also existed. This was furnished with a table and form, another table with two little chairs, two stools and three shelves. It was on these that his comprehensive collection of brass and pewter was been displayed. Around the grate was everything that was required for cooking. The buttery was still used for its original purpose, while the parlour and chamber were both bedrooms.

Husbandman John Buxton occupied the only five-roomed dwelling. This consisted of a houseplace and parlour with chambers over both, as well as a buttery. The houseplace, which appeared to be the only room with a fire, contained only a table, and the parlour only two beds. The chamber over the houseplace also contained one bed while the one over the parlour had a little table and a pair of bedstocks. In the buttery was his coppery ware. Unlike some dwellings where rooms had dual purposes Buxton's rooms all had specific functions with the houseplace used for cooking and eating, dairying performed in the buttery, and the other three rooms for sleeping. The only individual with six rooms was Husbandman Robert Sale. His property consisted of a houseplace, parlour, cheese chamber, buttery (not mentioned) with chambers over the parlour and buttery. His upper chambers were, as was common, combined areas for sleeping and storage.

Thomas Haslam had seven rooms consisting of a houseplace, parlour and kitchen, with chambers above each of these, as well as a chamber over the entry. The entry itself was unmentioned, usually being a hallway often found between the main body of the house and the kitchen. The houseplace contained a table and two forms, with chairs and stools. The parlour appeared to be the only dual-purpose room with a bed, press and coffer, along with a table, form and chair. The kitchen was used for cooking and the four upper chambers contained only beds and coffers.

Thomas Haines, a clerk, was also appraised with seven rooms and the only dwelling with evidence of recent rebuilding. The houseplace, buttery and old parlour were augmented with a new parlour and a new chamber. The only upper rooms were chambers above the houseplace and old parlour. The houseplace contained a table along with chairs and stools. It is possible that with the rebuilding the buttery had now become the kitchen as this was the only room to contain brass, pewter and iron ware. The new parlour appeared to act as an entertaining room with a table, cupboard and stools, while the old parlour had become a bedroom. The new chamber contained a bed and some old chairs, and the two upper chambers were both bedrooms.

Gentleman James Cresswell lived in a twelve-roomed property. These consisted of a houseplace, kitchen, parlour, buttery and backhouse, with chambers above each, as well as a cockloft and cellar. The principal room was the parlour containing nine leather stools, five buffet stools, two couch chairs, one child's chair, two ordinary tables, a livery table, a pair of tables and all the plate, along with cushions and carpets. The houseplace contained a table and two chairs, and in the kitchen was a table and form along with provisions and his brass, pewter and ironware for cooking. The buttery and cellar contained a variety of wooden ware along with bottles and earthenware. In the backhouse was the malt mill, backstone and furnace. Two other individuals also possessed malt mills and these are indicative of those who were likely to have been engaged in brewing. The chamber above the backhouse contained bags, winnow sheets and a haircloth. The other four upper chambers, two of which contained desks, were all used as bedrooms. The cockloft was furnished with the servants beds. Creswell's inventory was one of only two to mention reading material with books in his closett, the other being Ralph Adderley who possessed 'one wainscott box with a dictionary & other small schoolbooks in it'.

Gentleman Adam Colclough occupied the Delphehouse, a thirteen-roomed property in 14. This consisted of a hall, hall chamber, parlour, black chamber, little chamber, little passage, kitchen, store chamber, corn chamber, backhouse and cellars. Only three chambers, one over the parlour and two over the kitchen were specifically listed as being upper rooms. The inventory indicates that the property had five fireplaces, which is confirmed by the Hearth Tax taken 18 years earlier. These were in the parlour, hall, kitchen and two of the upper rooms. The parlour was the principal room for entertaining with 14 leather chairs, a table, livery cupboard, two carpets and items for the fireplace.

Carpets provided extra warmth for those that could afford them. These were either used to cover tables or as bed coverings rather than being placed on the floor. Carpets in the modern sense did not become common even in the homes of the wealthy until the last quarter of the 18th century. The hall was more modestly furnished with two tables, a chair and items for the fire. The kitchen contained a table, three chairs and three stools, along with all his cooking utensils and dishes, trenchers and flagons. In the cellars were stored barrels, tubs and other wooden ware, along with brass pans and earthenware. The corn chamber was empty apart from plough and wain timber. In the backhouse was a malt mill and ten strikes of malt, no doubt ready for the next brewing. The remaining six rooms were all bedrooms and all but one contained either chairs, stools or tables. Two of these also contained rugs. These were generally more coarse than carpets, and also used alongside sheets and blankets to provide extra comfort. The principal bedroom was the chamber over the parlour, being one of the two upper rooms that possessed a fireplace. Besides the featherbed and all its furnishings were two chairs, two stools, a looking glass and a livery cupboard. This last item was specifically for storing supper provisions and candles. The black chamber boasted the latest in privacy with a window curtain. Although curtains were commonly found in inventories these were usually part of the bedding furniture.

As well as the thirteen rooms of the main house were eight outbuildings including stables for his horses, cowhouses, an ox house, a waine house and a number of barns in which were found items of husbandry. His inventory was also the only one to mention items associated with mining, suggesting that he was the owner of an early colliery.

A True and perfect Inventory of all and singular the goods and chattells of Adam Colclough late of Delphowse in the parish of Dilharn in the Countie of Stafford gent deceased taken and apprized the seaventeenth day of March Anno Domini 13 by us Edward Doughty William Adderly and Thomas Rowley gentlemen

		£	s.	d.

Imprimis his purse and apparrell apprized att — 05-00-00

Item   in the parlour fowrteene leather cheires one table & frame
one liverie Cupboard two carpitts a paire of andirons fire shovell & toungues — 02-08-00

Item   In the hall two tables one forme one cheire one greate one pair of iron goberts — 01-10-00

Item   In the kitchen one table & forme three cheires three stooles
two iron drippin panns one iron morter three large old brasse kettles
two little brasse kettles three old brasse potts one warmeinge panne three spits
one little paire of Goberts a clever a skellett two tostinge irons twenty dishes
of pewter two fflaggons one chamber pott fowre dozen of trenchers — 07-12-06

Item   In the cellars six barrells two powderinge tubs two brasse panns
two tres earthen ware and wooden ware — 02-00-00

Item   In the chamber over the parlour one bedstead one matt one feather bedd
one bolster two pillowes two blanketts one counterpaine curtaines & valance
a couchsraine two stooles two cheires a liverie cupboard
a little lookinge glasse one carpitt one fire shovel & tonges — 06-03-04

Item   In the black chamber one bedstead one matt one featherbedd
one boulster two pillowes two blanketts one counterpaine curtaines & valance
three cheires two stooles a little table a window curtaine — 05-06-08

Item   In the hall chamber one bedstead one matt one featherbed
one boulster two pillowes three blanketts one rugge curtaines
& valance a little table fowre cheires three stooles — 04-10-00

Item   fowre & twenty paire of sheetes of fflaxon & hempen and ten paire
of course sheets five dozen of napkyns six cubbard clothes
six pillow beares three towells three table clothes — 06-02-06

Item   In the little passage a little feather bed one boulster
two blanketts one counterpaine — 01-10-00

Item   In the little chamber over the kitchen one bedstead one matt one feather bed
one boulster three blanketts one coverlid one cheire one cubbard six cushions — 02-03-04

Item   In the chamber over the kitchen one bedstead one matt one rugge curtaines
and valance two cheires two stooles a close stoole & fire shovell and tonges
one coffer one truncke some little boxes one old clocke — 02-13-04

Item   An old watch — 00-13-04

Item   In the store chamber about two hundred of cheese fowre fflitches
of bacon an old coffer a straw which and six cheese boards — 04-13-04

Item   In the corne chamber plow tymber and wayne tymber — 03-00-00

Item   In the backe howse two arkes two kinnells one mault mill
about 10 strike of mault — 05-05-00

Item   In the little stable one old white horse bridles and saddles — 05-00-00

Item   In the greate stable five old cart horses — 12-00-00

Item   Five paire of iron geares six collers nyne paire of harness two cart saddles
tenne bridles new and old three Iangwiths one locke a currey comb & brass — 01-10-00

Item   The hay in the barnes stables & cow howses and two rickes — 11-10-00

Item   Barley in the barne — 02-00-00

Item   oates in the barne — 04-00-00

Item   fitches in the barne — 01-00-00

Item   fowre oxen — 20-00-00

Item   fowre bullockes — 16-00-00

Item   In the wayne howse one wagon one wayne one cart two tumbrills
two harrowes two plowes and other Implements of husbandry
seaven yoakes fowre chaines wayne ropes — 20-00-00

Item   five cowes & calves seaven incalved cowes and heaffers — 12-00-00

Item	fowre steares	11-00-00
Item	five stirkes	10-00-00
Item	seaven calves	09-00-00
Item	A bull	03-00-00
Item	One forty and eight sheepe of all sorts	42-00-00
Item	boards and tymber	02-10-00
Item	In the chamber over the oxe howse an old bed and beddinge	00-06-00
Item	one hogge and two stoare piggs	02-14-00
Item	things forgotten & unseene	00-10-00
Item	three poore old gin horses	01-10-00
Item	post wood in the wayne howse and in the field two colepitt ropes nagars & other materialls belonginge to the colepitts and the gins	04-00-00
Item	the corne upon the ground being about three acres of Mastlin	09-00-00
		291-02-10

Apprized by
Samuel Adderley   Edward Doughty   Thomas Rowley

The largest property of the inventories that stated the names of rooms was that of gentleman John Hollins. His home boasted a hall and a room next to it, a parlour, parlour chamber, middle chamber, green chamber, kitchen, upper kitchen, buttery, little butter, larder, cellar, maids chamber, servant mens chamber, backouse, a little room at the end of the gallery (although the gallery itself was not mentioned), and a chamber over the kitchen. Like Adam Colclough, his principal room was the parlour. This was furnished with nine chairs, six turkey-worked cushions, a pair of tables and a short table, a livery cupboard, a clock (the only individual to possess one), a map and two short carpets. In the hall was a table, two forms, an old stool, a cradle, a going wayne for children (possibly an early version of a pram), a chest and a still.

The inventory shows us what could be found in a well-equipped kitchen. Besides the furniture, above the fire that burnt in its own grate was a spit, a jack and a pair of racks. Complementing these was a fire shovel, two pairs of tongs and a pair of bellows. There was also a pair of potracks, a dripping pan, dish kettle, warming pan and a skimmer. A number of brass items included two pots, two skillets, three little kettles and a ladle, along with 17 unidentified pieces of pewter. Also present were five porringers, two flagons, a cleaver, shreading knife, mortar and pestle, a salt and salt coffer, and a birding piece, this last item being a gun for shooting birds and fowl. A separate upper kitchen contained the wooden ware and next to this was the little larder used for storing earthenware. Also, in one of the cellars, were six Burslem milk pans. There was also an unspecified quantity of trenchers and spoons in a little room at the end of the gallery.

The green chamber, middle chamber and parlour chamber were all bedrooms, while the chamber over the kitchen, the maids chamber and servant mens chamber were all bedrooms of a lesser standard. His backhouse contained two malt mills and two stone cisterns. Both the buttery and little buttery were used for storage.

Footnotes

62. The area of jurisdiction of the parish constable.
63. The figure was divided by 3.29.
64. An exercise undertaken on the neighbouring parish of Caverswall revealed that using this methodology as a means of estimating the population was remarkably close to that produced by multiplying baptisms by thirty (413)
65. Finn, 'Possessions and Place in a Rural Community', p1.
66. No properties were recorded with 9 hearths.

8. Parochial Administration and Governance

Many aspects of 17th and 18th century governance may be found among the churchwardens' accounts.[67] It was the incumbent who was responsible for the morals and good behaviour of his parishioners, along with his churchwardens'. Their offices gradually evolved so that by the 16th century they were clearly defined with the major three being the village constable, the overseers of the poor and the surveyor of the highways. These were augmented by the vestry - what may be thought of as a local parliament, the forerunner of the parish council - with the authority to monitor the elected church officers to ensure they were proficient in their duties.

Churchwardens' and overseers were elected annually each Easter 'agreeable to the ancient and usual custom of this parish'. Some did serve longer but a vestry meeting in 1805 reiterated that 'it was unanimously agreed that for the future no officer shall be allowed to serve any parish office any longer than one whole year except chosen by a public vestry and not to serve by substitute without chosen by the vestry'. The term substitute affirms that qualification was based upon the occupation of certain properties. Even as late as the middle of the 18th century there were still entries such as 'The account of Jonathan Bradshaw, overseer of the poor, for William Kinsman's house from Easter 1763 to Easter 1764.'

Overseers were both unpaid and unpopular. It was they who would have to go around the parish and decide who should pay parish rates and how much. They would then have to return to collect what was due and distribute it to those who they considered were deserving and to refuse those they considered were not. By the beginning of the 19th century the vestry minutes record that there were ten overseers for the liberty of Dilhorne and the same for Forsbrook. It was also sanctioned that each of the two liberties should be responsible for paying and maintaining their separate and respective poor.

There were regular payments for the incumbent, sometimes accompanied by his sidesmen, for church court attendance fees at Caverswall, Cheadle, Uttoxeter and Stafford, as well as hearing briefs at Caverswall. Drink was often recorded in the accounts:

One quart claret and a pint of sack at Christmas	2s.8d.
Two quarts and a half drink and a pint of sack Palm Sunday	5s.
Six bottles of wine for Easter	10s.
Three pints of sack and five quarts and a half claret	11s. 9d.
Ale at a meeting	1s.6d.

Payments occasionally must have been considered excessive. It may have been partly due to this that the churchwardens' in 1703 declared 'and we all agreed that five shillings should be the limit always to be spent upon the parish accounts at Easter.'

Occasionally details of churchwardens' expenses as they performed their duties were recorded separately in the vestry minute books:

Thomas Loton's journey and expenses to Gnosall by his order	7s. 10d.
Ditto horse hire and Thomas Lotons time	9s.
My journey, horse and expenses to $2^1/_2$ miles beyond Gnosall and home again	10s.6d.
George Hammersley's expenses with me	2s.
Total	£4 4s.

Expenses were paid for perambulations of the parish boundary. This was an annual task undertaken by the churchwardens' to ensure that the boundary was still clearly defined. Any buildings that had appeared within the parish since the last perambulation would have been liable to pay taxes to the church. The accounts make sporadic comments to this function:

1693	Expense at Widow Buxtons for perambulation	3s.
1703	Spent for going the boundaries	3s.
1706	At perambulation	1s.
1709	A perambulation	1s.

Widow Buxton may have been the proprietor of an inn, or simply just a convenient meeting place after the boundary had been traversed. No doubt refreshment was provided after the task had been completed and it is interesting that the substantial reduction of expenses after 1703 corresponds with the agreement reached by the vestry recommending a limit to what was spent.

The destruction of vermin was also the responsibility of the churchwardens', with cash incentives offered to those who obliged:

1706	For a foxhead 1s.
1744	For 2 foxes 2s.
1767	To Thomas Heath for 4 fox heads 4s.

Although only payments for fox heads appear in the accounts it was also customary to offer bounties for the eradication of other vermin including badgers, weasels, polecats and even hedgehogs and sparrows. The humble but unfortunate hedgehog was thought to suckle milk from cows during the night, as well as being able to steal apples by sticking them to their spines. Sparrows, however, were a real threat through the damage they could cause to thatched roofs.

Footnotes

67. Although separate Overseers of the Poor accounts exist from 1733 some aspects of poor relief were still recorded in the general churchwardens accounts.

9. The Maintenance of the Poor

One of the major obligations of the parish was for the maintenance of its poor. This had been instigated by Parliament when the Poor Law Act was passed in 1601. This was introduced by central government who chose the make the parish responsible for their own poor and to act as the unit of administration.

It is often thought that the Act was introduced as a result of the dissolution of the monasteries sixty years earlier. Before the dissolution monasteries had often been a place where the poor could receive charity in times of hardship.

The Act was introduced for two different reasons. Firstly during the preceding century the population had almost doubled. Secondly there had been a steep rise in the level of inflation, possibly by as much as 500%, although wages had failed to keep pace. This increase in population, a large proportion of who were seeking work, reduced the cost of labour. As a result the living conditions of many fell dramatically. The accounts for Dilhorne reveal that payments would be made for those struggling financially, such as:

1716	Given Inskip 6d.a week for 50 weeks	£1-7-6.
1745	Paid Thomas Salt 10 weeks	10s.
1746	Paid Mary Salt 55 weeks at 1s per week	£2-15-0.
1753	Paid Mary Salt 3 months	14s.
1754	Paid Jonathan Salts wife	5s.
1803	John and Mary Crosley are allowed	4s per week
1806	Samuel Bamford is allowed	1s. per week and his bed repaired.
1807	Thomas Thorley is allowed	1s. 6d. per week and a shirt
1807	Ann Walters be taken from	3s. per week to 2s.
1807	Ann Walters is allowed	1s. per week and to have her rent paid as usual.
1908	Thomas Thorleys	3s. per week be stopped.
1808	George Hurst is reduced from 2s. to 1s. per week. Likewise he is allowed a shirt.	

For those on parish relief it appears that the average weekly pay ranged from one shilling up to six shillings. These cash payments were simple for the overseers to administer. However, the sums were not comparatively large. It is estimated that during the middle of the 18th century 1s. 6d. would be just enough to buy bread for one person for one week. As the last two entries reveal, payments were occasionally terminated although the accounts do not state a reason. Reductions or stoppages may have been the result of the individual gaining at least some part-time work thereby reducing their necessity for parochial relief. Long-term continual payments may have been the equivalent of pensions.

There were also payments for those who were unfit through illness to support themselves as well as medical expenses:

1703	Paid for bleeding Thomas Haines	1s.
1713	Paid Mary Harvey for washing Thomas Haines	3s.6d.
1713	Paid James Harvey for cleansing him	1s.
1725	Ann James in her sickness	1s.
1744	Gave Thomas Salt in his illness	1s.
1809	Paid to Mr Watson for Doctoring the poor of this parish.	

Pregnant women on parish relief were also allowed one pound five shillings for the expense of the lying-in month. Many, however, would have struggled back to whatever tasks they were involved with well before the end of the month. During the first week a midwife would have called each day to make sure that both mother and infant were comfortable.

There are numerous accounts of the parish providing and/or mending clothing for individuals. Where individual items were listed the most numerous were shoes, shirts and waistcoats:

1703	A pair of shoes for Thomas Haines 3s.4d.
	A pair of breeches for William James 1s.11d.
	A pair of clogs for William James 1s.
1710	For 8 yards of linen cloth to make 2 sheets and a frock for Thomas Hollins 4s.
	Paid to William Gurney for making William Haynes coat, waistcoat and breeches 2s.6d.
	For making frock, breeches and waistcoat for Richard Hammersley 1s.6d.
1752	Two shirts for Bettanys two lads 2s.
1764	To Hammersley's coat cloth 7s.
1785	A pair of stockings for Lydia Wright 1s.8d.
1803	Widow Wheawalls son Charles is to have a shirt and a pair of shoes, and her daughter Ann is to have some clothing.
1806	Ann Fernihough is allowed a pair of shoes and a petticoat.
1806	Ordered 2s. for Margaret Plant shoe-mending.
1807	Hannah Thorley is allowed a shirt, a petticoat, a bed gown and 6d. per week.
1807	William Wheawall is allowed a flannel pair of breeches.
1808	Samuel Lowe is allowed a shirt, a waistcoat and a pair of breeches for his son and a shift and a slip for his daughter, and each of them a pair of shoes.
1809	Samuel Bettanys wife is allowed a petticoat and 1s. 6d.
1809	Thomas Salts wife is allowed 5s. towards clothing her children.

This latter entry is one of many where parents would claim that they were unable to clothe their children. In addition to clothing, sheets and blankets were also commonly-provided by the parish. In 1810 John Whitehurst was also able to receive a chaff bed along with two blankets.

Applications for items other than money or clothing included numerous entries for coal. From the amount of payments for November 1802 it would appear that this was an exceptionally cold month. Other items included:

1767	John Wheawall 2 pecks of meal	1s.3d.
1808	Daniel Bettany is allowed two measures of potatoes.	
1810	Paid for an ass for John Wright the elder	2s.6.
	Robert Heath to buy hay for his cow	3s.
	Straw for Thomas Perkins and for fetching the straw from Draycott	1s.6.
	Robert heath for going to fetch the straw and for the softening of it	2s.

For those who could not afford to pay for funerals these expenses would also be met by the parish:

1687	Paid at the funeral of a poor woman	1s.
1703	For the burial of Thomas James	8s.2d.
1707	Paid for a coffin for a poor traveler 4s, meat and drink at his funeral	3s.4d.
1710	For George Hollins wife's funeral	10s.
1716	For the burial of James Cook	10s.
1722	Fred Balls child's coffin	2s.6d.

1754	Paul Viggars funeral	10s.
	Burying Edges child	7s. 4d.
	Burial of Old Lucas	6d.

Why the burial of Old Lucas cost so little is unknown. Possibly the costs were part-met by relatives or friends, or possibly he was just unpopular. There also appeared to be payments for festivities including entries for 'wedding food' and 'eating and drink when married' showing that providing sustenance for guests was an important part of the ceremony. Nothing appears to have been overlooked, even down to 'a cabbage for the workhouse 1d'.

Sometimes the cost of repairs to an individuals dwelling would be met:

1687	Paid to William Hollins for building Amy Hollins house £1-10-0.
1706	Paid to repairing Jonathan Leeses house 16s.
1710	Paid for a house for Jonathan Jayne £3-3-0.
1717	For repairing Ann Shaws hovel
1726	Andrew Hurst for house room for him after his gable end fell, 8 weeks, 2s.6d.
1728	For repairs towards Robert Heaths barn
1810	John Spillsbury is allowed 2,000 bricks towards building his house.

Most, if not all of these dwellings were thatched, as payments for thatching also appear intermittently throughout the accounts. By the middle of the 18th century it appears that the average thatcher earned between 2s. and 2s. 1d. per day, although for dressing he would only be paid 4d. All but the last entry predates the parish workhouse. The entry for Andrew Hurst demonstrates that some of these buildings were less than substantial.

It is possible to trace through the accounts different events for the same individuals and to paint a very brief picture of their existence, usually towards the end of their lives:

1689	Paid Amy Hollins her pay	£1-2-6.
	The twelfth of October she was buried	
	Paid for the coffin and carrying her to church	
	Paid to the ringers	
	Paid to John Fernihough	
	Paid for lying her in the coffin.	

1714	Paid Ellen Amtrey 14 weeks pay 10d. per week	11s.8d.
	Given her in her sickness	1s.
	Paid for her coffin	4s.
	William Cope for her burial	1s.
	Paid to the clerk	6d.
	Paid for fetching the bier	6d.
	Paid for tending her and laying her out	1s.

Three consecutive entries appear for 1764:

1 load of coal for Sarah Myott	7 1/2d.
1 months pay for Sarah Myott	4s. 8d.
Paid to Sarah Myotts funeral	3s.[68]

On March 31st 1752 the parish agreed that 'no person or pauper within the aforesaid parish shall receive any payment except by wearing a badge of letters of red cloth on the right arm marked with D.P. and in case the officer of offices does not pay any of the aforesaid persons or paupers their weekly pay a house rent shall be fined according to an Act of Parliament in that case and one further mind is that the aforesaid parishioners and paupers shall be badged within the limitation of one month after this date'.

A later entry records 14d. of cloth to letter the poor. The Act referred to dated from 1697 being 'An Act for supplying some Defects in the Laws for the Relief of the Poor.' Badging the poor this way may have acted as a deterrent due to the stigma attached but also prevented people from fraudulently claiming charity elsewhere or undertaking paid work. Those who refused to wear the letters risked losing their relief or in some cases whipped and set to hard labour for three weeks.[69] Not all parishes complied with the Act and eventually the practice was discontinued at the beginning of the 19th century.

The not insubstantial sum of providing outdoor poor relief was a constant drain upon parish resources. To help combat this on 29th January 1735 the churchwardens' and overseers of the poor agreed to have - ' a convenient house ...for employing all such from the parish of Dilhorne as shall desire to receive relief from the same'. An inventory of the workhouse, as it was then referred to by the vestry, taken in April 1737 records its contents:

Three chaffe beds
Two chaffe bolsters
One feather bolster
One feather pillow
Nine blankets
Nine sheets
Four pairs of bedsteads
Two chairs
Six stools
Two little wheels
One iron pot
One iron kettle
One gaune
One stean
One grate
One frying pan
One pair of tongues
Three noggins
One bag
Twelve pewter spoons

The appraisers also mentioned that one chair and four stools were also wanting. Those in the workhouse would have been set to work. Mostly these tasks would have included spinning and weaving. If the workhouse had a farm attached then they would have been engaged in agricultural tasks. There were regular payments for woollen and linen cloth, together with coat buttons and crest buttons. It is possible that these were materials for those in the workhouse. There were also sporadic references to the upkeep of the parish house including its thatching. However, outdoor relief still seemed to be available after the workhouse had been built as the following entries reveal:

1741　　　Edward Chell four weeks for keeping six poor £1-4-0.
　　　　　Four weeks for three heads and keeping Mary Fletcher £1-14-4.
　　　　　Eleven weeks for three heads at 13d. each £1-15-9.
　　　　　Two heads, three weeks at 2s. 2d. each 6s.6d.
1744　　　Mary Challinor for a weeks table for Elizabeth Stevensons child 1s.6d.

These entries suggest that the overseers contacted out the provision of some of their poor, possibly because accommodation at the workhouse had already reached its capacity. Although workhouses existed there were still provisions for boarding out children and responsible persons. Those who were willing and able to work were not always brought to the workhouse, as sometimes the guardians would secure employment for some, possibly subsidising any deficiencies in their wages.

Many individuals had their rents paid, either for the whole year or half-year, or for an unspecified period, although these payments were similar to yearly or half-yearly amounts:

1803 Mr Collier agrees to pay to Joseph Warrilow out of his own pocket than to have him in the house
1805 Lydia Whitehurst is allowed £1 1s. towards her house rent
1806 Thomas Bettany is allowed 10s. towards rent.
1806 John Shufflebotham allowed £2 towards his house rent.
1807 William Rushtons house rent is to be paid to Phillip Johnson £1-15-0 due May 1st 1807.
1808 Thomas Inskip is allowed £1-9-0 towards his rent.
1808 Thomas Bettany is allowed £1-4-0 per year towards paying his house rent to Mrs Holliday.
1808 Thomas Bettany is allowed £1-5-0 for half a years rent.
1809 John Mills is allowed £1 towards his rent.
1810 Matthew James is allowed half a years rent £1-2-0.
1810 George Wheawall gives his three houses up to the parish paying to him 3s. per week.

Possibly the workhouse was temporarily full in 1803 when the vestry ordered that Rebecca Saunders, Elizabeth Beatey, Rebecca Denies, Hannah Bridget and John Rushton having each of them a house to themselves at the expense of the parish [shall] be put together in one house at the expense of the parish. That the vestry could order individuals into the workhouse is evident from entries such as:

1803 Ordered that Mary Fernihough is to go to the workhouse or have no pay.
1807 Ann Tomkinson is to be taken to the workhouse at Caverswall or to have no pay.
1808 Lidea Whitehurst, wife of Thomas Whitehurst, is to have no pay and she is ordered to the workhouse.

Where the workhouse was located is unknown. It would not have been a substantial building and probably looked similar in appearance to many of the other dwellings in Dilhorne during this period. Some that were not in the workhouse were allowed to at least attempt to earn a living on their own means with equipment provided by the parish:

1805 Margaret Plant is to have a pair of woolcards.
1805 Ellen Wood is allowed a pair of cards 2s. 6d.
1806 Thomas Thorley is allowed a spade, a pair of shoes and no pay until they are paid for by his one shilling and six pence per week.

Woolcards were used to turn tangled wool into fibres to make the wool ready for spinners and weavers. These examples indicate that the overseers believed that by providing these unfortunate individuals with the necessary equipment they would be able to earn enough to support themselves to a certain degree.

Although the primary concern of the churchwardens' and overseers was for their own parishioners they were also charitable to outsiders:

1689 Given a poor man by Hollins order 6d.
1692 Given a poor man with a paper 3d.[70]
1707 Given a widow that came from Lincoln 1s.
1711 Taking a poor woman by john Whitehursts order 1s.6d.
1713 A seaman 1s.
1716 Paid for carrying away a sickman 6d.
1717 A travelling woman 1s.

1721	Charges with 2 travelling women and 4 children 3s.2d.
1744	Paid to a Birmingham woman 10s.
1803	An assessment made and allowed at 2d in the pound on all the houses, gardens and old enclosed land within the parish of Dilhorne for a man that was deficient in the army of defence agreeable to an Act passed for that purpose.

This last entry possibly relates to a maimed soldier. Paying for somebody to keep moving was better in the eyes of the overseers than having someone stay indefinitely and thereby being a larger financial burden. There were also collections for disasters elsewhere, known as Briefs. These were Royal mandates issued for deserving causes and read from the pulpit at the end of the service:

> Collected for the great fire at Bungay [Norfolk] the sum of five shillings.
> Heden in Yorkshire, loss by fire   99s.
> Havant in Southamptonshire, loss by fire   52s. 40d.
> Kanely in Lancashire, loss by fire   2s. 6d.
> The church decade [decayed] at Chester   2s.
> For Repair of the church at Portsmouth   2s.

These were intended to help with the costs of rebuilding the churches and there would often be separate collections for the poor sufferers at these places.

Not all charity was provided by the overseers of the poor. To the left of the doorway hangs the board recording those who left charitable bequests for the less fortunate of the parish. These are found in most parish churches, often dating from the 18th century, although sometimes incorporating earlier bequests. These requests were entrusted to the incumbent and the churchwardens' for administration. The board lists a total of twelve bequests. Five of these state the actual sum left, normally to be invested, the interest gained then paid out to those who qualified. The remaining seven listed the actual amounts to be distributed, ranging from between 10s. and 20s. Five bequests were as a result of investment in lands, and five named the individuals who were charged with their administration.

Other bequests would have been administered and disbursed by the overseers. Two bequests, rather than being distributed annually, were paid out twice a year. Five of the fourteen dates stipulated for distribution were on St Thomas's Day with a further three on Good Friday. St Thomas's Day on July 3rd was one of the most popular days for disbursement. This may also have a correlation with the St Thomas's Trees area above the church, or that the church had originally been dedicated to this saint. The remaining dates were St Andrew's Day, St John's Day, Candlemass Day, Christmas Day, December 27th, and New Years Day

A TABLE OF BENEFACTORS TO THE POOR OF DILHORNE PARISH

Mrs Jane Hollins by will left £20 the interest thereof to be annual distributed on Good Friday forever[71]. Copwood Hollins esquire her brother left £40 the interest to be distributed on St Thomas's Day yearly forever. The sums are now in the hands of Mr Thomas Harrison of Dilhorne Hall. John Gill by will gave 20 shillings to be distributed on two days in the year viz Candlemass Day and St Andrew's Day forever, charged upon Lady Birch & Lady Birch Meadow in Dilhorne in the hands of Samuel Adderley esquire. The said Samuel Adderley by will charged the same lands with the further sum of 20 shillings to be distributed, 10 shillings on St Thomas's Day & 10 shillings on Good Friday. [Blank space left as if a Christian name was possibly going to be added at a later date] Whitehall gave 10 shillings per year to be distributed on St Thomas's Day forever, charged on a moiety of the Wheat Ley in Forsbrook. George Wood left 10 shillings per year to be distributed on St Thomas's Day forever, charged upon Pike butts in Forsbrook. Mr Richard Warner late of Chatham, left £10 the interest thereof to be distributed on Good Friday forever, now in the hands of Mr Richard Warner of Forsbrook. Mrs Charleston left 10 shillings per year to be distributed on St Thomas's Day forever charged upon lands called the Marl crofts adjoining to Callyhill Estate. Mr John Boulton by will dated May 2nd 1713 left £10 the interest thereof to be distributed on St John's Day forever, now in the hands of his son Mr George Boulton. George Turnock by will dated 22nd August 1727 left 15 shillings per year to be distributed the next New Years Day after the decease of the survivor of John Turnock of Lower Tean and Sarah his wife, forever, charged upon his house & croft in Forsbrook. Mr John Covill by will left on his Estate in Dilhorne, the sum of 10 shillings per year to be distributed the 27th day of December forever. Mr Samuel Bamford Esquire left £100 invested in the funds, the interest to be distributed on Christmas Day forever.

During the second quarter of the 19th century Dilhorne, along with many of its neighbouring parishes[72], was incorporated into the Cheadle Poor Law Union. This was formed following the Poor Law Amendment Act of 1834. The workhouse in Cheadle had been built in 1775 replacing an earlier one that had been in existence since at least 1761. This was enlarged four years after the creation of the Poor Law Union in 1838 so that it was capable of accommodating 150 paupers. This two-storey building with a T layout still exists on the south side of Bank Street. This was augmented in 1902 with a three-storey infirmary and a cottage home for pauper children. These stood immediately south and south-west of the workhouse respectively. Of the 104 paupers recorded there on census night 1881 only three were from Dilhorne.[73]

Footnotes

68. Dilhorne Churchwardens Accounts SCRO D5/A/PC/3.
69. Tate, W. E., 'The parish Chest', p193.
70. Probably a settlement certificate.
71. This is stated in her will dated 7th November 1679. The spinster left her estate divided between her two sisters (£40 each), her father (£20), sister-in-law (£10) and a friend (£5). She also willed her wearing apparel to her two sisters. The £20 that she left to the poor she stated that the interest was to be given to the poor every Good Friday 'distributed by the discretion of my executor or his assigns together with the minister of the parish', and nominating her brother Copwood Hollins as executor.
72. The fifteen parishes incorporated into the Cheadle Poor Law Union were Alton, Bradley, Cheadle, Cauldon, Caverswall, Checkley, Cheddleton, Consall, Cotton, Denstone, Dilhorne, Draycott, Fradley, Ipstones and Kingsley.
73. Joseph Inskip an unmarried 60-year-old farm labourer; Joseph Whitehurst, a married 78-year-old sawyer; and another Joseph Whitehurst, a 74-year-old married farm labourer.

10. Illegitimacy and Settlement

The overseers of the poor were keen to be exempt from the maintenance of illegitimate children. For mothers who gave birth to illegitimate children, as if the stigma and humiliation was not enough, they were often whipped or sent to the house of correction for a year. The overseers may have attempted to persuade the reputed father to marry the female in question before the birth of the child, thereby transferring responsibility for the maintenance of the child. This was even more attractive if the father was from outside the parish, whereby responsibility was transferred.

If this was not possible the overseers would have to generate an order for the upkeep of the child from the local Justice of the Peace or at the Quarter Sessions. This, however, would have involved court fees, transport and accommodation costs for usually three people while the bastardy bond was produced. The advantage was that the father could be punished, including imprisonment, if he failed to keep to the terms of the bond.[74] This bond could be either a lump sum, or a series of installments to the overseers.

A convenient but harshly cruel reality was that it was not unknown for the mothers of illegitimate children to murder their offspring, the excuse offered to enquiring parties that they had experienced a stillbirth. The overseers would not have pursued the matter with little or no evidence, especially as this was one less burden upon parish funds. The overseers accounts for 1746 include 'for a travelling woman who came bigg bellied and getting her off to Caverswall.. 5s'.

A Bastardy bond dated December 28th 1738 concerns Mary Salt. Mary had been born in Cheadle but appears to have settled in Dilhorne. Still unmarried, she had recently given birth to a male bastard child. Upon being examined under oath by Caesar Colclough, Justice of the Peace, she had stated that Henry Bradshaw, a tallow chandler from The Hollins at Kingsley, was the father. The obligation bound Bradshaw, along with John Hollins and William Froggatt, both also from Kingsley, for the sum of £100 'as insurance against all manner of expenses, damages, costs and charges whatsoever which shall or may at any time hereafter... [be made]... of the said Mary Salt's said bastard child and to provide the maintenance, education and upbringing of the child.'

A similar bond exists for Elizabeth Salt of Dilhorne, who in 1703, was 'lately delivered of a male bastard child called John Salt alias Wheeleton'. The obligation named John Wheeleton of the parish of Stoke as the father, who, along with Samuel Alcocke of Rownall in the parish of Cheddleton, were bonded to prevent the child becoming chargeable on the parish.

Not all illegitimate births appear to have been covered by a bond. In 1807 the overseers offered one individual the opportunity to make weekly payments, an early form of child maintenance. Allen Martin was to pay 2s. 6d. per week, otherwise to pay £45 or to give a bond to indemnify the parish from a child fathered upon him by Ann Brambley belonging to the parish of Dilhorne. The CSA was not a 20th century invention.

Exactly who belonged to a particular parish led to a certain amount of confusion. To combat this problem Settlement Certificates were issued to individuals. The parish of settlement was the parish that the individual had been born in, which also applied to illegitimate children, the only exception being wives who would take their husband's parish as their parish of settlement upon marriage. Settlement could also be obtained through apprenticeship within the parish, or through being in service for more than a year. Disputes over settlement resulted in

Settlement Examinations, taken before a Justice of the Peace or at the Quarter Sessions court. Settlement certificates must have made the parish feel as if it were a prison. In some respects it re-introduced the notion of the old ways of the individual being tied, not to the Manor this time, but rather the parish.

The majority of settlement certificates are often extremely detailed. Some individuals were from outside the parish claiming settlement because they had either been apprenticed or because their parents had been born in Dilhorne. Some also claimed to have been born within the parish themselves. Many individuals were from neighbouring parishes such as Caverswall and Draycott. The furthest included individuals from Stourbridge and Warwick. They reveal that some individuals were extremely mobile when seeking employment and that work for some was seen as a series of contracts rather than a long-term career. Below are three paraphrased examples of individuals seeking settlement in Dilhorne:

The examination of James Bolton, labourer, taken upon oath before Thomas Parker and Caesar Colclough esquires, two of His Majesties Justices of the Peace on the 26th day of September 1733. Bolton had been born in the parish of Dilhorne and that eleven or twelve years ago, to the best of his remembrance, lived as a servant to William Foard of Cookshill in the parish of Caverswall for the term of twelve months. After this he hired himself to Richard Woolf of Stansmore Hall, Dilhorne, for the twelve months. Sometime after this he was hired as a servant for eleven months by John Hollins of Bucknall. Since then he was hired by Thomas Tabernor of Stone for a term of eleven months. After this he was hired for a year by James Finney of Blakehall but only served half a year. Since that time Bolton said that he had not been hired, had not served any office or paid any levies, or rented any tenement of ten pounds a year.

The examination of Philip Hawkins taken upon oath before me Ralph Sneyd esq., one of his Majestys Justices of the Peace the sixth day of march in the year of our Lord 1759. Hawkins said that he had been born at Roughcote in the parish of Caverswall where his father rented [property and land worth] about fifty or sixty pounds a year. About the age of thirteen he left his father and was a hired servant with James Capy of Blythe Marsh Mill in the parish of Dilhorne from May Day to Michaelmas. Afterwards was hired with him for eleven months at the expiration of which time he was hired for eleven months more. Following this he went and hired himself with Joseph Lovatt of Cresswell Ford in the parish of Dilhorne for eleven months and three weeks but left him before the eleven months were expired and went to live with John Gosling of Cresswell Mill in the parish of Draycott with whom he was hired for eleven months at the expiration of which time he received his wages and was hired with him for eleven months and three weeks and so on from time to time for about the space of five years. During this time he married a wife named Eleanor but has not paid any levies nor rented any tenement of the yearly value of ten pounds nor served any parish office or done any other act or thing whereby to gain him a legal settlement.

The examination of James Tildesley, labourer, then residing at Norbury on the 5th June 1830, when aged 49, taken before Edward Buller. Tildesley said he had been born in Norbury where his parents were legally settled. When he was between the age of 15 and 16 he was hired to Thomas Tildesley, farmer, of Pickstock Brook in the parish of Chetwynd, as a waggoner for twelve months. He entered into service the day before New Years Day and left before the following New Years Day. To the best of his knowledge he had not done any act whereby he would gain a settlement in his own right. In the year 1800 he was married at Dilhorne to Maria Thorley by whom he had two children born after marriage. In 1803 he went for a soldier and has never seen his wife since that he has heard and believes that his wife received relief from Chetwynd parish for several years after he went for a soldier and he has also heard and believes that his wife is now living in the parish of Dilhorne with one Rupert Gallimore and has a family of children by him.

Once the parish of settlement had been decided upon then certificates would be issued so that individuals could show that they would not be a financial burden to any other parish except their own:

To the Churchwardens' and Overseers of the poore of the parish of Dilhorne in the said County.

We whose hands and seales are hereunto sett and subscribed, being churchwardens' and overseers of the poor of the parish of Carswall in the said County, doe hereby own and acknowledge Thomas Inskip and Sarah his wife to be legally settled in our said parish of Carswall, and that we and our successors will at any time hereafter receive them back into our said parish of Carswall whenever they shall ask reliefe of your said parish of Dilhorne, unless they shall acquire a settlement elsewhere according to Law; as witness our hands & seales this eleventh day of May Anno Domino 1724.

The document is signed by six names, then countersigned by two justices of the peace.

The vestry minutes make occasional references to individuals being removed from the parish such as in1805 when it was 'Ordered that Thomas Heath Howell, the son of James and Jane Howell, shall be immediately removed from the parish of Dilhorne to the township of Charlesworth in the parish of Glossop in Derbyshire'. However, no reason is stated why Howell was removed or if any expenses were incurred. Three years later they ordered that if Joseph Buckley and John Martin 'do not reimburse the parish of Dilhorne from the expenses occurred concerning the removal of Mary Buckley they shall be removed from out of the parish of Dilhorne to the parish they belong'.

Just as the overseers of Dilhorne were keen to remove those who did not have legitimate settlement, so to were the overseers of other parishes. In 1758 the overseers of Uttoxeter ordered the removal of William Heath, a button-maker, along with his wife Mary and their four sons John, Thomas, William and Richard to Dilhorne.[75] In 1771 the overseers of Cheddleton issued an order for the removal of Hannah, Margaret and John, the children of John Bagnall from their parish back to Dilhorne. No indication is given as to why only the three children should be removed and the decision of the overseers to theoretically divide the children from their father seems somewhat harsh.[76]

Footnotes

74. Tate, W. E., 'The parish Chest', p217.
75. Staffordshire Record Office, Q/SBe/22/44.
76. Staffordshire Record Office. Q/SB 1771A/2.

11. Crime and Punishment

The first recorded crime in Dilhorne occurred in 1272. Agnes, the widow of Nicholas de Dulverne, appeared before the County Court accusing Richard le Roper of Abbots Bromley, along with three others, of beheading her husband. At the trial it appeared that Nicholas had stolen a horse and would not stand to the Kings Peace[77] on demand of Richard and the others who then beheaded him.[78]

This is not as peculiar as it may first appear due to how communities were policed. Most males between the ages of twelve and sixty were obliged to become a member of the tithing, a group responsible for upholding the law in their community. Dilhorne and Forsbrook, together with outlying hamlets, would have had their own tithings. On discovering a crime they would be responsible for raising the hue and cry as an alert to summon other tithingmen. If the crime was serious enough a group of armed men known as a posse comitatus would pursue the criminal until being caught. If he attempted to evade arrest the posse comitatus had the authority to behead the accused providing that a coroner was present and that they had not reached the sanctuary of the local church. In theory anyone fleeing the law had the right of sanctuary within a church for up to forty days. In reality angered pursuers, possibly including relatives of the injured party, frequently dragged the criminals out to either apprehend them or to administer their own justice.

In 1307 Roger, the son of Hugh le Mouner of Dilhorne, killed Richard de Staunton in Dilhorne and had fled as an outlaw.[79] Outlawry was punishment for a serious crime, particularly when the accused refused to appear to answer charges brought against him. From this point the accused was a lawless man, literally outside of the law, with loss of civil liberties and rights. His goods were, and often his real estate, seized by the Crown. He would be referred to as a Wolf's Head, and like wolves, could be killed upon sight.

In 1308 Walter Hogshawe took William Amotson to court for causing waste and destruction in lands, houses, woods, and gardens in Dilhorne. Hogshawe had previously demised to Amotson a messuage, two carucates of land, ten acres of meadow and eight acres of wood in Dilhorne. Hogshawe claimed that Amotson had wasted them by digging pits in six acres of land and selling the marl and clay to the value of 100s., and pulling down a Hall worth £20, and selling the timber, two chambers, each worth £10, a kitchen worth 100s., a grange worth £10, an ox stall worth 40s., and cutting and selling 300 oak trees each worth 2s., 300 lentistos, each worth 12d., forty apple trees each worth 2s., and twenty pear trees each worth 2s. for which Hogshawe claimed the substantial sum of £200 in damages. Six years after this Ralph Basset senior of Cheadle was accused of causing waste and destruction in the lands and houses which he held in Dilhorne.

In 1319 Roger, the son of Henry de Caverswall, accused Richard Albeyn of coming with arms into Dilhorne and cutting down his trees to the value of 100s., and beating and ill-treating his servants.[80] Three years later Richard de Dulverne and twenty-one others were accused of coming with swords, bows and arrows to Draycott where they had insulted, beaten and wounded Ralph de Shepeye for which he claimed £100 in damages.[81]

In 1329 Robert de Caumpedene, the vicar of Dilhorne, was being sued by Richard de Leghes, for forcibly taking two oxen worth 40s. from Dilhorne, 28s. in money and other goods and chattels belonging to de Leghes to a total value of £20. Caumpedene did not appear when requested to answer the charges. The sheriff was ordered to arrest Caumpedene and place him in exigend, the first process to being outlawed.[82] Fearing the worst Caumpedene absconded and was deemed an outlaw.

In 1354 Hugh de Stanton sued Ralph Prestone of Dilhorne for depasturising cattle on his growing wheat at Dilhorne, and for insulting, wounding and ill-treating his servant Margery de Stanton, claiming that as a result he had been deprived of her services.[83]

Neighbourly issues continued when in 1367 Peter de Caverswall was in dispute with William de Pressale for entering his free warren at Dilhorne, cutting down his trees and taking hares, rabbits, pheasants and partridges without his permission.[84]

In 1396 Ralph Galpyn was accused of wasting tenements demised to him by Thomas Beek by digging and selling marl and clay from two acres to the value of 40s., and by pulling down and selling the timber for 10 marks, and by pulling down two chambers each worth £40, a kitchen, and a stable each worth 40s., and cutting down and selling from the wood forty oaks each worth 4s., sixty ash trees each worth 3s., and by cutting down in the gardens, one hundred corulos[85] each worth 8d., twenty pear trees each worth 4s., and twenty apples trees each worth 6s., for which Beek claimed £200 as damages.[86] All these examples of 13th and 14th century crimes show another side of Merrie England in a quiet backwater. Most were against property rather than individuals. Those who fled the law rather than face justice may never have seen Dilhorne again.

Two centuries later any crimes deemed less than serious were dealt with at the Court of Quarter Sessions, so called because it sat four times a year. The Quarter Session Rolls for Easter 1652 recorded that Anne Bullock of Forsbrook was accused of attacking Mary, the wife of John Clows, in Dilhorne Church during a service in a dispute over pews. Pews were introduced into churches during the 17th century. Before this parishioners either stood or squatted on the floor during services, while the elderly would lean against the walls, or use simple benches introduced during the 14th and 15th centuries. In a rural settlement such as Dilhorne the ownership of pews was with properties in the parish rather than individuals and would descend as such. The seating pattern reflected the social hierarchy of a community where the rich sat at the front, the middling classes in the centre and the poor at the back or against the sides. The church, ever mindful towards its congregation for its financial upkeep, began renting pews to increase funds. To occupy someone else's pew was almost seen as a form of trespass as Mary Clowes may have discovered.

Arguments with individuals from neighbouring communities would sometimes result in violence. On May 5th 1771 four individuals from Dilhorne - Thomas and Samuel Adams, along with John Martin and Ralph Gallimore, armed themselves and went to Caverswall where they broke all the glass in the windows of William Poulton's house. Lesser offences included Sarah Challinor in 1772 who was accused of stealing a linen cap belonging to George Wright.[87]

A later incident concerning the theft of potatoes was recorded in a handwritten statement by the Justice of the Peace:

County of Stafford

The Information and Complaint of Samuel Salt of Dilhorn [sic] in the same county, collier, taken and made before me John Holliday esquire, one of His Majesties Justices of the Peace for the said county the eighteenth day of September in the year of our Lord one thousand seven hundred and ninety seven who on his oath saith that Thomas Mellor of Blakeley Bank in the parish of Dilhorn aforesaid did on or about the fourteenth instant, steal and take away potatoes in a basket which potatoes had been sown or planted near to Blakeley Bank by and were the property of Samuel Salt and that the said Thomas Mellor on being charged therewith confessed that he had taken about a quartern of potatoes from the place aforesaid.

Taken and sworn the eighteenth day of September 1797 before me
[signed] John Holliday.
The mark of Samuel Salt [X]

On the same piece of paper an affidavit confirmed:

Zachary Wright of Dilhorn aforesaid labourer maketh oath that he saw Thomas Mellor taking up and carrying away from the place abovementioned potatoes which he put into a basket and that the said Zachary pursued him within about forty yards of the house of the said Thomas Mellor.
The mark of Zachary Wright [X]
Sworn the 18th of Sept before me [signed] John Holliday.

That same day Holliday sent instructions to the special constable of Dilhorne, John Spilsbury, that Mellor was summoned to appear before Holliday at Dilhorne Hall on Wednesday 20th September at 9am. Mellor was convicted of the crime which occurred the previous Thursday. Even though Samuel Salt's potatoes were only valued at 6d. the penalty inflicted on Mellor was 7s.6d.

The vestry minutes of 1797 recorded that the churchwardens' of the Forsbrook division were required to put up in some wide or open part of the town a pair of stocks to be kept in good order with a lock thereto - 'and that the stocks at Dilhorne be forthwith repaired and put up near the gate of the churchyard westward and kept in good order with a lock.' This was a continuation of an ancient custom, probably originating from the time of the tithingmen, where those thought to have committed petty offences would be subjected to a mixture of punishment and humiliation. With their feet secured in the wooden frame they would be pelted with all manner of rotten vegetables and fruit together with verbal insults.

The first reference to some form of regular policing was recorded at a vestry meeting of 1803 when three men had been sworn in at Leek as members of the militia for Dilhorne. In 1810 a note in the vestry minutes records that John Cashmore shall be proceeded against for Sabbath-breaking as the law direct. Later the toll house at the junction of High Street and Sarver Lane served as the police house.

Most petty crimes continued to be dealt with by the Quarter Sessions Court. The following give a flavour of the business of the court during the early 19th century:

1815 Samuel Rushton, aged 35, obtaining under false pretenses a jacket and 7s. 6d. with intent to defraud William Titley of Dilhorne.

1816 Benjamin Moore, aged 40, for want of sureties to answer his having begotten Ellen Broad of the parish of Dilhorne, singlewoman, with child of a bastard.

1817 George Hurst, aged 26, stealing two fowls the property of Joseph Thorley of Dilhorne.

1817 Ralph Whitehurst, aged 35, for leaving his family chargeable to the parish of Dilhorne.

1820 Joseph White, aged 24, for stealing a smock-frock, a pair of breeches and a handkerchief, the property of George Baker and Elizabeth Baker of Dilhorne.

1822 John Bestwich, aged 23, arrested on suspicion of stealing a one pound Uttoxeter banknote from Thomas Thorley of Dilhorne.

1830 Mercy Hemmings, aged 16, obtaining from Samuel Jackson at Dilhorne by false pretenses 40 oz worsted, one ham, one shoulder of bacon, 2 doz of fancy buttons and one pair of bootlaces, his property.

1834 Charles Morecroft Beardmore, aged 13, accused of stealing six geese, the property of Thomas Thorley of Dilhorne.

1834 Joseph Hurst, alias Malkin, aged 29, stealing 5s. in copper coin the property of Mssrs Bamford and Co. at Dilhorne.

1842 Thomas Johnson, aged 28, maliciously wounding Samuel Barlow with intent to do him grievous bodily harm. Convicted of assault and to be imprisoned eight months and kept to hard labour.

The most bizarre crime recorded in Dilhorne was that of Thomas James. At the Summer Assizes on May 18th 1811 James, a 60-year-old labourer, was committed for a felony at Forsbrook. He was condemned and sentenced to be executed.[88] The crime he was accused of was bestiality with an ass. The conviction appeared to have been secured by the evidence of Thomas Inskip, and despite the evidence he gave being classed as conclusive various doubts existed. James himself derided Inskip's character and several attempts were made to secure a pardon based upon the unsavoury character of the principal witness.[89]

Those are the facts as they exist. What follows are details of the story which cannot be verified but which are purported to be true. The incident was supposed to have occurred on the afternoon of Friday May 9th. Three days later Inskip made a statement to the Rev. E. Powys claiming that while walking near the Stone House he saw James following a female ass into a field. He observed that when James caught up with the ass he took his genitals out of his trousers and inserted them into the ass. When the ass moved forward James genitals fell out and again he inserted them. Inskip claimed that he challenged James but that James ignored him. Inskip then went up to see if the genitals of the ass were wet, which he said they were.

A few days earlier James had caught Inskip beating his dog with a stick. He forced Inskip to stop and then threw his stick away. Fred Johnson of Forsbrook witnessed Inskip being verbally abusive to James and saying that he would be sorry for interfering. Unfortunately Johnson was never called to give evidence.

The day after his initial statement Inskip returned to Powys to add that he had also seen sperm on the ground where the incident happened. Powys tried to dissuade Inskip, questioning his story's authenticity and suggesting that he had possibly made a mistake, also informing Inskip that the ass may have been wet if she was in season although Inskip still insisted it was due to James.

On May 16th Inskip visited Powys a third time, who was accompanied by two other justices of the peace, Mr J. Hulme and Mr. W. A. Coyney. This time he added to his statement that the sexual act between James and the ass lasted between one-and-a-half and two minutes.

Two days later James was summoned to appear at Blythe Bridge police station in front of Powys, Hulme and Coyney. When the allegation was read out James thought it was a joke. He was asked where he was at the time of the offence and told them that he had been at Cheadle market. When asked if anyone could verify his story he said that there were lots of witnesses. He also related the story of the dog beating and Inskip's threats of revenge. Asked if anyone could verify this he told them about Johnson. However, neither Johnson or those who had been at Cheadle market were asked to give statements. Instead James was arrested and charged at Stafford.

Although James told the court that he was at Cheadle market at the time of the offence, and of Inskip's threats against him, the judges refused any witnesses to give evidence. All that James said was ignored and the jury delivered a verdict of guilty. Although he protested his innocence, and a petition for leniency, James was given the death penalty.

The Staffordshire Advertiser reported the execution of 31st August the following week:

On Saturday last Thomas James convicted at our assizes of a crime against nature, suffered death on the new drop in front of our county gaol. We understand from the clergyman who attended him after condemnation that he resolutely protested his innocence and did not fail to arraign the character of his prosecutor to his last moments. James was an elderly man, and has left a family to lament his ignominious fate and the overwhelming shame and sorrow of the circumstances of his death. He was remarkably resigned to his fate during the latter part of his time; and told his wife that if she did not demand his corpse and give him a descent burial, he would, if it were possible, visit her again. His body was accordingly demanded by his friends and consigned to the grave with as much respect as the circumstances of his friends would allow. He walked with a firm and steady step from his cell to the lodge but spoke not to anybody after the clergyman left him. Several applications were made to procure his pardon from considerations of the character of his prosecutor, but without effect.

Three months after the execution Inskip confessed to the landlord of the Cross Keys in Cheadle that he never intended to send James to the gallows, only wanting to teach him a lesson for interfering. He admitted that he had made the whole story up. The landlord dutifully repeated the confession to the police. Inskip was prosecuted for committing perjury and sentenced to three months imprisonment. This, of course, was little compensation for James, or his family who were left behind.

By the middle of the 19th century the regular police force had been established. The enrolment of paid officers employed by local councils rapidly replaced the authority previously held by parish constables.

Footnotes

77. The 'King's Peace' refers to the general peace secured to the entire realm by the law administered in the King's name.
78. Assize Roll, 56 Henry III, 1272 in SHC Vol. IV, p211.
79. Gaol Delivery, Edward I, 1305.
80. Plea Rolls, Edward II, 1319.
81. Plea Rolls, Edward II, 16 Easter (1322).
82. Plea Rolls, Edward III, 1329.
83. Plea Rolls, Edward III, 1354.
84. Plea Rolls, 1367.
85. Corulos or Tally.
86. Plea Rolls, Richard II, 20, 1396.
87. Indictment against Sarah Challinor, wife of John Challinor of Dilhorne, labourer, for stealing a linen cap, property of George Wright, 1st Jan, 1777 [sic]. Staffordshire Record Office. Q/SB 1772 A/17-22/21.
88. Staffordshire Assizes 1811 Calendar.
89. William Salt Library, Standley, A. J., 'Stafford Gaol', typed Mss, p46.

Blakeley Bank from the churchyard.

The toll house which later became the police house and is now a private dwelling.

Early 20th century view of the building at the entrance to the original road that ran from the Royal Oak in the direction of the church. This was later diverted and renamed 'New Road.' The building was two separate houses at the front and a third at the back
Photo courtesy of Aubrey Salt.

Modern view of the above building.

12. Communications

The only major road running through the parish is that which skirts its southern extremity at Blythe Bridge.[90] Built by the Romans, this connected their forts at Derby and Chester. The upkeep of roads was the responsibility of the parish in which they ran, and overseen by a parochial officer known as the surveyor of the highways. Both local taxes and labour were required to keep the roads in a useable condition. With the increase in traffic many parishes were simply unable to fulfil these obligations. The answer lay in the formation of separate trusts to take over the maintenance of particular stretches of road as well as building new ones. This operated by levying a toll for those using the road with fees being collected at toll houses situated along the route.

The road from Derby to Chester was turnpiked in 1759 and managed by the Uttoxeter-Newcastle Turnpike Trust with travellers having to obtain a token at the Swan Inn, Blythe Bridge.[91] However, two years later it appears that the overseer of the highway for Dilhorne was still responsible for the maintenance of the part of the road that passed through the parish:

> For mending Blythe bridge
> For a plank 8ft 4s.
> For a pound of spike nails for the sides 4d.
> For the work 1s. 2d.   (2nd January)

In 1762 an Act of Turnpiking the road from Blythe Marsh through Forsbrook to Thorpe via Cheadle and Oakamoor was passed. The course of the original road was altered where it now begins to climb to Boundary so that it skirted the Red Lion Inn and continued, not to Brookhouses, but to Four Lane End. This stretch of the old highway was known as Warrilows Lane and ran almost parallel with the lane that now leads from the cottages at Boundary to Commonside and onto Huntley. From its junction at Four Lane End it was possible to continue to Huntley, turn left for Brookhouses or right for Draycott Cross.

A two-storey octagonal toll house was built on the junction of Cheadle Road and Dilhorne Road in 1829, and a turnpike gate also existed at Town End Brassworks Company.[92] The toll house at Forsbrook was finally demolished in the 1950s when the road was widened. From the junction at Four lane End it is possible to retrace a portion of the original route running towards Boundary although becoming lost before reaching the Red Lion.

During the 1780s an application for turnpiking another road through the parish was met by opposition, mainly from mine owners. Admiral John Levison Gower, on a visit to Dilhorne Hall, declared that he would rather be in the Bay of Biscay, in a storm, than on one of Dilhorne's coal roads in a carriage. The opposition eventually subsided and the Bill passed into law.[93] The road was eventually turnpiked due to the amount of coal being transported through the village and a toll house built at the junction of Sarver Lane.

The securities to the turnpike were owned by Sir Edward Manningham Buller who restyled the Toll House in the 1860s. When the tolls ended the property reverted to his Estate. In 1873 an agreement was made between Sir Edward and the Chief Constable of Staffordshire to rent the house for use as a police station. The rent was five guineas pa which remained the same until the house was sold in 1919 as part of the first Dilhorne Estate sale.[94] At the sale it was purchased by Enoch Dale. He renamed it Homeleigh and rented it to Rupert Mosley and his wife who moved from the old Mosley family farmstead of Day House Farm, a Georgian farmhouse in Sarver Lane.

Sometime during the 18th century the course of the road running from the area around the

Royal Oak to the church was altered. This stretch of roadway is known as New Road, which is something of an anomaly as the road skirts the churchyard wall and is probably the oldest road in the community. Unfortunately the earliest maps of sufficient detail show its current course.[95] However, two clues suggest that originally this may have run in a more direct line from the Royal Oak towards the church. The earliest maps suggest the possibility of a T-junction. Possibly this was stopped up by the occupiers of the Hall extending their parkland or simply because those responsible for turnpiking the road through the community considered the present route more acceptable. Also, the large house that now stands adjacent to the Royal Oak[96] is built to face a main road, rather than presenting its gable end as it currently does. That this dates from the early 18th century indicates that the original route of the road was still used at this point.

Yates map of Staffordshire in 1775 shows these roads with the exception of the one that leads up to the Common from the Royal Oak. Upon reaching the Common the road appears to terminate rather than continuing along its current course to Boundary, which is also omitted from the map. It is likely that this existed as a trackway along its current course.

The map also contains a number of other anomalies. Although Dilhorne and Forsbrook are portrayed as having the same amount of dwellings, those in Dilhorne appear to stretch along from the junction with Caverswall Lane to the junction leading up to the Common. However, a contemporary watercolour (previously discussed for showing a late 18th century view of the Hall) shows this area without dwellings. Since the cartographer appears to have taken great pains concerning accuracy it is unusual that the buildings were placed in this location. As well as Boundary being omitted so too is Godley Brook, although smaller outlying farmsteads including Kelson, Callyhill (sic) and Magdale (sic) are shown.

However, by the time of the first Ordnance Survey map, compiled from surveys taken between 1817 and 1837, both Boundary, along with Daisy Bank, and Godley Brook were included. The road along the Common to Boundary is clearly shown, as is another that ran from near the crossroads at Boundary, past Blake Hall to New Close Fields and continued to Adderley.

Although never coming to fruition, during the 1790s the benefits of a canal linking to the main Trent and Mersey was also considered. This would have reduced the cost of the transportation of coal by half, which by road was almost 1s. a ton per mile.[97] Another proposed method of communication came in 1877 in the form of a passenger railway. The proposal was a route running from the main Stoke to Derby line to Cheadle. This was to branch from the main line just after it crosses the bottom of Stallington Lane in Blythe Bridge to run north through Blythe Marsh, curving through the centre of Forsbrook and then in a straight line to Blakeley Bank. From here it turned north-eastwards to Whimpney Wood and then south-east to Dilhorne Colliery, passing Old Engine Farm, and then across the Forsbrook to Cheadle road between Delph House and Brookhouses to enter Cheadle via Majors Barn.

Footnotes

90. The Cheadle to Cellarhead road forms part of the northern boundary of Dilhorne parish.
91. Pointon, Matthew E., 'A History of the Parish of Draycott-en-le-Moors, p96.
92. Chester, Herbert A., 'Cheadle Coal Town', p51.
93. Letter to Stebbing Shaw, 1797. William Salt Library. MI48.
94. During its period as a Police House occupants included Police Constables John Waldron, Sylvester and Stevens.
95. Yates' Map of 1775.
96. Numbers 10 and 11, The High Street.
97. Letter to Stebbing Shaw, 1797. William Salt Library. MI48.

**The remains of the original road that ran to the church
before the New Road was built.**

New Road skirting the wall to Dilhorne Hall.

13. Industry and Occupation

Before, and even during the first part of the 20th century, the majority of people worked where they lived, or at least in close proximity. Now the opposite exists as most inhabitants of rural settlements are employed outside of where they live, commuting to nearby towns and cities. Many of these settlements may now be thought of as commuter suburbs. Similarly, before the beginning of the 20th century most people were employed in agriculture or an associated trade. Less than 2.5% earn their living in this way now.

The outcrops of coal that were available meant that mining was undertaken from an early date. As previously mentioned the name Dilhorne originates from Dulverne, meaning a place of digging or delving. Coal was mined for blacksmiths and for the furnaces used for burning lime. Because conventional chimneys had yet to be incorporated into domestic dwellings burning coal indoors resulted in smoke and unpleasant fumes. It was not until the 17th century with the advent of smaller fireplaces with efficient chimneys that coal would be burnt in the home. Whatever was mined was used locally as coal was not a commodity that was easy to transport great distances due to the condition of the roads.

The first documentary evidence of coal mining was in 1371 when Ralph Freman of Rollesley sued William Cade of Dilhorne for forcibly entering his coal quarry (quarry carbonum) at Dilhorne, as well as for mowing and carrying away his hay, and for taking fish and coal from the quarry to the value of £20. Cade did not appear when summoned to answer the charges and the sheriff was ordered to place him into exigend and if he failed to appear to decree him an outlaw.[98]

Outcropping continued although by the 19th century this method had been superseded by larger mines. Local landowners now became coalmasters, with those who prospered most being those who exploited their land for non-agricultural use. One of the most industrious local landowners was Edward Bamford of Park Hall. The Bamfords had occupied a site at Park Hall on the parish boundary with Cheadle since at least the 16th century. Another was Adam Colclough who lived at the Delphe House, the son of Sir Caesar Colclough, and whose probate inventory has already been discussed.

When Adam married Elizabeth Bamford, two of the leading gentry families became united. Adam's daughter Jane went on to marry William Adderley of Blake Hall. The Adderleys had been one of the most prominent families in Dilhorne since the 15th century. A generation before John Whitehurst of Whitehurst had married an earlier Elizabeth Bamford from Park Hall. Had this quartet formed a partnership it could have governed the coalfield much earlier than when Samuel Bamford took control in the 18th century.[99] By this time the Bamford family had built 'a most handsome mansion' at Summer Hill, near Bank Top.[100]

An agreement of 1753 exists between Edward Bamford and Simon Mountfort of Beamhurst Hall. The Mountforts, another prominent family, had already started to mine in the New Close Fields area and retained their partnership with the Bamfords for the next eighty years.[101] This was until 1830 when the 50-year lease was terminated by the mine owners claiming that Bamford and Mountfort had not complied with the terms of the agreement. Mountfort, then set about working his own teams of men around Blake Hall[102] - the following year Blake Hall Colliery opened under the ownership of Henry Mountfort of Beamhurst Hall[103]

The Dilhorne Colliery started operating in 1774. This was equipped with modern steam engines on a site now known as Old Engine Farm.[104] Another colliery was situated at Park Hall

Foxfield Colliery which closed in 1969.

Foxfield Colliery.
Photo courtesy of Mick Faulkner.

(slightly outside the parish and manorial boundaries, being in Cheadle) on the site of the Bamford family's ancestral home. There were numerous smaller workings undertaken by single individuals. Herbert Salt[105] 'worked at getting coal on Madge Dale and The Dale' in 1867.[106] Charles Salt[107] was proprietor of the Dilhorne Common Colliery in operation between 1867 and 1877. He also worked the 'stinking coal' at Whimpney Wood in Dilhorne.[108] Stinking coal was considered inferior to normal coal. The unpleasant smell given off during burning was caused by a large proportion of sulphuret of iron. This was also mined at Coalbrookdale in Shropshire for the sole purpose of burning lime.[109]

The largest colliery in the parish, and of the Cheadle coalfield as a whole, was the Foxfield Colliery which was in production for more than eighty years. A shaft was sunk in 1880, originally known as Mann's Pit after the two owners, brothers John and Enoch Mann. By 1893 production had necessitated its own branch line connecting it to the main railway line three miles away at Blythe Bridge. Other railworks included the tramway laid out between New Close Wharf, through Dilhorne Colliery (Old Engine), to a wharf on the road above the present Godley Brook Chapel. Later the tramway was extended crossing the road to connect with the lower end of the Foxfield Railway line.[110]

Foxfield was modernised during the 1930s and production from the nearby Park Hall Colliery transferred.[111] The government nationalised the coal industry in 1947 and Foxfield entered a further period of expansion. By 1954 the workforce totalled 550 and produced 210,000 tonnes of coal a year.[112] However, decline set in and in 1965 the mine was closed by the National Coal Board. Before the end of the decade the branch line running to Blythe Bridge was taken over by the Foxfield Light Railway Society.

The government report by Samuel Scriviner in 1841 on 'The Employment of Children and Young Persons in the Coal Mines of North Staffordshire and on the State, Condition and Treatment of Such Persons' gives an insight into the working lives of those employed in the mines during the mid-19th century. Interview No.22 was Joseph Salt[113], aged 54, examined on March 20th.

I am a buttie collier; have worked in Delph House 12 years and more for Mr Holmes; I contract for the 'Old Sawney' and the 'Litley' pits; I employ about a score men and near 10 boys in the two pits; the youngest is about 12, I cannot say exactly. I engage to deliver coals on the bank to the master at 3s. a ton, sometimes it is more, never less; 12 or 13 years ago it was but 10s. 2d. The price rises or falls proportionate to the men's wages, which wages are regulated by the demand for labour; it has, however, been almost a regular price for the last 30 years. I have never known it vary more than 4d. a day, and that only for a short time. We are now drawing nine to ten tons a day, before now I have drawn 20 tons and more than that. The men under me are paid pending upon the number of men employed; the average of men's wages is 3s. per day; the boys are paid in a like manner, they having to draw or drive so many corves; their wages vary from 8d. to 2s. 6d. per day according to their strength and age, from 10 years to 18. They draw or drive on rails; the bottom is soft and slushy; the height of our mainways varies from three to four feet, but it is always changing, as the earth is constantly rising. I have seen the mainways hove up clean full, stopping up air and everything in a few weeks. I have never known any fire-damp, wildfire, or sulphur in the pits. We get plenty of choke-damp or black-damp, which we get rid of by good circulation, by lighting big fires at the bottoms of the up-cast shafts, or if that should not be enough we pump water down the down-cast shaft and create a draft through the roads or addits. I have never known any death result from either foul air, or machinery, or defective ropes. About four years ago a little boy fell down the pit from the top by handling a corve which he had no business to do; he was killed: he was no pit lad. I began to work when I was seven years old; had no other education but at night and Sunday-school, where I learnt to read and write, which I have found of great use to me in every respect as a collier and a Christian. Having seen and known these advantages myself, I am a great advocate for the education of our youths now-a-day. As it regards those who work in our colliery, I am very glad to say that they have been very well looked to; all of them can read and most of them can write; every one of them attend Sunday-school; if there is an exception I do not know it. They work the same number of hours with the men, that is, from six or seven to three or four, very seldom 12 hours. There are night sets occasionally, from six at night till two or three in the morning. This is the result of circumstance; at times there may be choke-damp, or machinery may be out of order; it is not a regular thing to work at night. I think they enjoy as good health as any boys, very different to factory children; they are never punished, or suffered to be by anybody. The men behave well towards them. I have been, as I said, 12 years at work here, and if I were required to be put on my oath I could say, that I have never seen one of our men stop a days work from drunkenness: it is not the practice for them to swear or be disorderly.

  (Signed) Joseph Salt

  Mining, however, was only one form of employment within the parish and there were other trades an individual could enter into. The Statute of Apprentices of 1563 forbade anyone entering into a trade without first serving an apprenticeship of (normally) seven years. To legalise matters apprentice indentures were introduced. These were legally binding documents that bound the apprentice to their master with a premium paid by the parents, or in the case of paupers by the overseers of the poor. In the latter case this was a gamble on the part of the overseers who hoped that their investment would be rewarded by the individual remaining in the parish after his apprenticeship and establishing themselves in their trades. There are occasional references in the churchwardens' accounts of individuals entering into an apprenticeship:

  1710 Jonathan Wood apprentice paid to his master £5.
      For binding him and his indenture 4s.
      For clothing him 5s.

  The apprentice received board and lodgings as well as his training. During this period the individual was not allowed to marry or to begin his own business.

  Forty-three Apprentice Indentures exist for Dilhorne between 1712 and 1843 - 28 boys and 15 girls. Their ages ranged from as young as seven up to fifteen, although the majority were between ten and twelve. The majority were for farming and husbandry (18), and other trades included tailor (5), cordwainer, housewifery (both 3), miner (2), and a blacksmith, joiner, stocking weaver, shade spinner, and flax dresser (each 1), as well as one individual with the dual occupation of hair-dresser and chair-maker. Five of the indentures failed to state an occupation.

  A note in the vestry minutes of 1800 recorded that 'the children of the poor parishioners shall be regularly put out to proper trades and services as soon as reaching proper age, and that no parent of any child who obstinately refuses shall not receive any weekly pay except unless expressly ordered by a magistrate to the great benefit not only to this parish which is heavily burthened [sic] with poor but also to the children themselves'. A number of entries in the vestry minutes reveal that this was put into practice:

  1803 Charles James is to have Wheawalls daughter as a parish apprentice, the boy to the Reverend
     Mr Wolfe if he is agreeable.
  1805 Ordered that James Lovatt shall be put out as a parish apprentice or have no pay.
  1805 Alice Harvey shall be put out an apprentice or to have no pay.
  1805 Hannah Barnes granddaughter shall be put out an apprentice or to have no pay.
  1807 Ordered that Mary Sharratt is to be put out prentice or have no pay.
  1807 Ordered that Thomas Day shall be apprehended for absconding his farming.

Many other references reveal the standard procedure of parish relief being stopped if an apprenticeship was refused. The last example of Thomas Day was unusual, possibly gaining employment elsewhere.

During the 19th century occupation was thought of as a vocation and therefore reflected social status rather than simply a description of economic activity.

Until the 19th century England was still largely an agrarian society, with wheat and oats being grown in Dilhorne since before the end of the 13th century.[114] However, during the 18th century the old method of communal farming came to an end. An Inclosure Act dated 1781 exists for Dilhorne[115] offering the opportunity for an increase in individual diversification. It was mainly the landowners and larger farmers that gained most from enclosure. So too did some smaller ones as they obtained more compact and easily-managed holdings no longer subjected to the rules of communal agriculture previously imposed but now under individual control. Some land doubled or even trebled in value alongside becoming tithe-free. Those who did lose out were the very small farms due to smallholders having to give up part of their land to compensate the tithe holder for the abolition of tithes or the building of new roads to give access to the adjusted land. For some this resulted in an acreage too small to be profitable. As the commons were enclosed the right of grazing enjoyed by many also became lost.

Even in 1881 it was still agriculture, rather than mining that formed the main occupation in the community, with eighty-six people employed in the former and only twenty-eight in the latter. There were a total of forty Farmers[116] including three with dual occupations[117], stating 'farmer and builder of 40 acres employing 9 men', a 'farmer and publican with 50 acres' and a 'farmer and assistant overseer'. A further four stated farming as their secondary occupation - 'butcher and farmer of 17 acres employing one man', 'green grocer and farmer of 9 acres', 'wheelwright and farmer of $4^{1}/2$ acres', and 'publican and farmer'. Others employed in farming were agricultural labourers, farm servants, farm bailiffs and a dairymaid. These figures do not take into account the wives, sons and daughters of farmers who no doubt contributed labour in some form.

The survey of employment based on the 1881 census is immediately after the agricultural depression of the 1870s. This was largely a delayed reaction of the repeal of the Corn Laws thirty years earlier when not only corn, but also meat and dairy produce, fruit and vegetables, were cheaper to buy due to imports from abroad. Before this a quarter of all men aged over twenty were employed in agriculture.[118]

Many agricultural workers were employed on an annual basis at hiring fairs. The most convenient hiring fair to travel to during the 19th century was the one that took place at Cellarhead. This occurred twice a year on May 5th and November 11th at the flat open area between the crossroads and Withystakes. The location was chosen because it lay at the junction of two main turnpike roads, the Cheadle to Cellarhead road that continued onto the Potteries and the one from Stone to Leek. Situated midway between these four places it attracted people from all of them, as well as from in-between. Those seeking employment would wear a straw token in either their hat band or their bonnet to indicate their availability to prospective employers. Negotiations would be entered into, including wages and conditions, hands spat on and a vigorous handshake to bond the contract.

Agricultural labourers worked from six in the morning until six in the evening during summer, and from seven, or first light, during winter. Often they lived in tied cottages, or directly with their employer in his house or one of the outbuildings. They would have had their own plot of ground in which to grow vegetables for their own sustenance. This may also have been true of those employed in non-agricultural occupations, the more industrious may even have kept a cow or grown a small amount of cereal crops. By the end of the 19th century the majority of houses were no longer sparsely furnished as mass-produced household items made in the industrial cities could be purchased in nearby towns. Similar to preceding centuries, their diet consisted of a heavy reliance upon bread which was eaten with butter, cheese, milk, mutton or bacon. Potatoes, augmented by a roast or meat pie, was another common meal. Although tea-drinking had become widespread beer continued to be the common drink. Agricultural workers were generally still low paid when compared to rural craftsmen, those employed in the mines and other industrial workers. This, together with a lack of housing in Dilhorne, would have been the reason to cause many to migrate to the nearby towns, in particular those of the Potteries, in search of alternative employment.

The total acreage farmed in Dilhorne in 1881 was just over 2,200 acres. The largest was Thomas Heaton of Stansmoor with 191 acres. Heaton, who had been born in Cheadle, had a wife and two young sons both under the age of five. Because of this two farm servants and one domestic servant were hired to help with running the farm. The census does not reveal any assistance from others who may have been employed by Heaton but were not living on his farm.

It should also be remembered that the census was taken in early April and extra help would have been required during the busiest periods of the farming year.

John Shoebotham at Callow Hill farmed 183 acres. Both he and his wife, who had been born in Dilhorne, were now in their sixties with only one unmarried daughter at home. Like Heaton, this meant that Shoebotham also employed two farm servants and one domestic servant.

If enough children were still at home this sometimes meant that employing outside help was unnecessary. Mary Pattson, a forty-nine year old widow at Blakehall farmed 173 acres. She had two unmarried sons and two unmarried daughters to assist her with the running of the farm.

Acreage farmed	No. of farmers
0-20 acres	13
21-50 acres	10
51-100 acres	7
101-150 acres	3
151-191 acres	4

Table 7. Acreages farmed and number of farmers recorded on the 1881 census

The table shows that a considerable difference in the acreages farmed existed. There were seven people with ten acres or less. These small farmers would most likely have kept pigs, hens and one or two cows producing eggs, milk and cheese for the market at Cheadle or the expanding pottery towns. Farms such as these would only provide a living if supplemented with other work.

Besides agriculture and mining the other most numerous occupational group was those employed as domestic servants (27). These were followed by those employed in the brick-making or brick-laying trades (12), dressmakers (12, including one milliner), general labourers (10) and the carpentry trades (8, consisting of two carpenters, two joiners, three wheelwrights and a cratemaker). Nine individuals were classed as annuitants (pensioners) and eight were retired.

The majority of wives were listed without an occupation, although this does not mean that they were unemployed. Women sometimes worked on a casual or part-time basis sometimes from their own homes that went unrecorded by the enumerators. This was common during the 19th century with the home being a place of production of articles or services. In the case of farms wives and daughters would have contributed labour. The family consisting of an independent male breadwinner with dependant wife and children was an ideal to which only a few could aspire. The wages of the head were often irregular and periods of unemployment or illness could cause acute crisis for the majority of families, few being able to save to meet temporary losses of income. From the reccurrence of surnames it is obvious that Dilhorne was a familistic community and it is possible to assume that the high numbers of kin would have been a source of assistance during times of hardship. The census records the sons of farmers, and other trades where sons followed their fathers occupation included two butchers, two brickmakers and two miners, a shoemaker and a miller. The youngest individuals employed were all aged thirteen, being a male farm servant and two female domestic servants.

Footnotes

98. Plea Rolls, 1371.
99. Chester, Herbert A, p15.
100. Pitt, William, 'Topographical History of Staffordshire', 1817.
101. Chester, Herbert A, p32.
102. Chester, Herbert A, p77.
103. Chester, Herbert A, p78.
104. Chester, Herbert A, p40.
105. The son of Joseph and Mary Salt.
106. Chester, Herbert A, p98.
107. Son of Great x4 grandfather Samuel's elder brother John.
108. Ward, in his geology of the Staffordshire coalfield, used this information given by Mr Salt's son. Chester, Herbert A, p101.
109. Penny Cyclopaedia of the Society for the Diffusion of Useful Knowledge, p286. http://books.google.co.uk (accessed 20/10/10).
110. Chester, Herbert A, p65.
111. This lay slightly outside the parish.
112. Chester, Herbert 'The History of the Cheadle Coalfield.' Landmark Publications (2002).
113. Joseph was the son of Samuel and Elizabeth Salt (nee Wheston).
114. Plea Rolls, Edward I, 1297.
115. Staffordshire Record Office. D30/2/7/115/12. This appears to be mainly for Dilhorne Heath and Haywood Grange.
116. Those classed as farmers that stated an acreage included the following sizes: 3, 4, 6Ω, 7, 8, 10 (x2), 12 (x2), 13, 15 (x2), 17, 24, 26, 28, 29, 30, 35, 40, 48, 50 (x2), 57, 60 (x3), 70, 84, 87, 104, 133, 140, 165, 173, 183 and 191. One of these employed one man, one employed one man and one boy, and another with the dual occupation of farmer/corn merchant (as well as stating that he was the Wesleyan preacher) employed 4 men.
117. In total ten individuals had dual occupations and a further two had three occupations.
118. Mingay, G. E., 'Rural Life in Victorian England', p17-18.

Dilhorne Hall from near the old rose garden.

The rear of Dilhorne Hall showing the servants quarters.

14. Population Analysis
of the 19th Century

At the beginning of the 19th century over three-quarters of the population of England lived in rural settlements. This has now been reversed with less than a quarter living outside urban areas. This does not mean that rural settlements have dwindled to non-existence. The natural increase in population during the last 200 years has seen a rise of those living in rural settlements from $6^{1/2}$ million at the beginning of the 19th century to over twelve million now.

The population of the whole parish in 1811, inclusive of the township of Forsbrook, along with Blythe Marsh and part of Blythe Bridge, was 1,184 inhabitants (581 males and 603 females) in 242 dwellings.[119] In 1851 the population of Dilhorne was 736, while that of Forsbrook was 143.[120] The figure for Forsbrook appears to be abnormally low, especially considering the growing community at Blythe Marsh. Possibly this was because the majority of inhabitants fell within the newly-created parish boundary of Forsbrook, rather than Dilhorne.

By 1881 Dilhorne (excluding the township of Forsbrook) had a population of 741 in 155 dwellings[121] with a further 19 uninhabited. The Census Enumerator's[122] route began at Robeys Bank, Bank Top and Whitehurst, then down to Godley Brook and walking up Godley Lane to include Sarver Lane before turning up to The Common. He continued to Boundary and Daisy Bank before going down the Cheadle Road to turn Back towards Godley Brook at Brookhouses.

He then walked up Whitehurst Lane to count the remaining dwellings on the moorland before returning to the village via Tick Hill, Blakeley Bank and the area around the church, recorded as Church Dilhorne[123], finishing at the Royal Oak. The census returns reveal much about the structure of the community during the 19th century. However, it must be remembered that the information is simply a snapshot of the population at a specific time (in this instance, the evening of April 3rd 1881). For example, households of elderly couples will not reveal children that may have reached adulthood and moved away.

That Dilhorne was a dispersed settlement with numerous outlying farmsteads is clearly demonstrated by the census. Sixty-six of the total of 173 dwellings were outside of the main settlements.[124] What may be thought of as the hub of the settlement around the Royal Oak and including Sarver Lane had a total of thirty-two dwellings. The area around the church from the junction with Caverswall Road to Dilhorne Hall that the enumerator recorded as Church Dilhorne contained seventeen. Godley Brook including Godley Lane had twenty-seven, and Boundary together with Daisy Bank had thirty-three.

The largest household was that of John Whitehurst of Whitehurst with eleven, all of who were family members with the exception of one domestic servant. The Whitehurst family of ten was one of the largest in the district although households of up to seven were common. John and his wife Emma had seven children at home between the ages of five and twenty-three, as well as John's father now aged eighty. The average family size was 4.25, slightly smaller than in the nearby pottery towns.

Of the total number of occupied dwellings - 155, excluding Dilhorne Hall - 112 were nucleated families, while forty-three were extended - those with family members other than the sons and daughters of the head of the household.

Extended Family Members (Total 67)			
Grandson/daughter	28	Father/Mother	3
Nephew/Niece	10	Mother-in-Law	2
Brother/Sister-in-Law	7	Step-daughter	2
Brother/Sister	7	Adopted daughter	1
Brother/sister	7	Great Niece	1
Son/Daughter-in-Law	5	Stepson (Head)	1

Table 8. Extended Family members showing relationship to the head of household

Grandchildren were the largest group of extended family members, followed by nieces and nephews, brothers and sisters, brothers/sisters-in-law and sons/daughters-in-law. Collectively they accounted for 9% of the population, lower than that of Caverswall, whose largest group was also grandchildren.

Non-Family Members (Total 57)			
Servant	31	Apprentice	3
Visitor	9	Boarder	2
Other	7	Lodger	1
Housekeeper	4	Nurse child	1

Table 9. Non Family members showing relationship to the head of household

Servants formed the largest group of non-family members within households[125], as in Caverswall. Most families employed only one or two, only two families had three, while one had four. Only thirteen of the thirty-one servants were true domestic servants, the remaining eighteen being live-in farm servants assisting with agricultural tasks. John Whitehurst's family of ten employed only one servant on his 104 acre farm while George Hill, with his wife and only two children, employed two. Hill's children were too young to help with the sixty-acre farm, Whitehurst's children had reached adulthood. Indeed, Whitehurst's servant Elizabeth Salt was specifically stated as being a domestic servant and may have contributed little or no labour towards agricultural work. Similarly Thomas Heaton of Stansmoor with 191 acres employed two farm servants and one domestic because his own children were too young to contribute.

Visitors formed the next largest group - only one was identified as being a relative of the head of the household. Visitors were from different parts of the country although two gave their birthplace as Dilhorne.

Seven people were classed by the enumerator as 'other' - meaning no definable relationship to the head. However, this figure is heavily biased by forty-two year old Keziah Harvey of Daisy Bank. Although married her husband was absent, and the other five inhabitants, all with the Harvey surname, were probably her offspring.

Four people were classed as housekeepers, all of who were employed by male bachelors or widowers over the age of sixty.

Of the three apprentices two were employed by blacksmith Henry Loton and the other by tailor James Bagnall, all three teenage males.

It should be remembered that the census only reveals those apprentices who were living with their master and disguises those who were living with parents.

There were two boarders and one lodger. The difference was that a boarder ate at the table of the household along with the family whereas a lodger ate separately and had his own distinct living space. Mary Jones, a nineteen year old assistant mistress boarded with schoolmaster Thomas Chadwick and teacher Alice Brassington at the school. The other was a seventy year old butcher living with a married couple in their forties. It is possible their children may have left home and taking in a boarder offered an increase to the family income. The only lodger was a fifty year old labourer staying with a brickmaker and his family.

Of the total of 741 individuals, 387 had been born in the parish of Dilhorne. Of those from outside 210 were from other areas of Staffordshire, the most notable being Cheadle (51), Caverswall (46), Cheddleton (17), Ipstones (8), Uttoxeter and Stone (both 7), Kingsley (6), Checkley (5) and Alton (4). Surprisingly there were very few from Cellarhead, Consall and Tean (each 3), Draycott and Wetley Rocks (both 2) and Fulford (1) considering their close proximity. Forty individuals came from the nearby pottery towns of Stoke on Trent. The remaining fifty came from other areas of Britain, not surprisingly a higher number from the neighbouring counties of Derbyshire (8), Cheshire and Shropshire (both 5), although there were also high numbers for those from Yorkshire (10) and Lancashire (9, including 4 from Manchester).

Taking only the 155 heads of households, sixty-eight had been born in the parish, sixty-four were from other parts of Staffordshire, and six from the nearby pottery towns of Stoke on Trent.

Twenty of the twenty-eight individuals employed in mining had been born in Dilhorne. Others came from relatively nearby, the furthest being from Butterton. Of those eighty-six employed in agriculture only thirty-two had been born in Dilhorne. This figure ignores those who were classed as retired or where farming was an obvious secondary occupation. Like miners, immigrants were from relatively close, all from within the county with the exception of one person from Macclesfield in Cheshire. The most numerous were those from Cheadle (12), Caverswall (8) and Cheddleton (4). Of the forty individuals listed as farmers only sixteen had been born in Dilhorne but all were from relatively close with the exception of one individual from Shropshire.

Of the 155 households 115 were occupied by married couples. Twenty-six of these were where both the husband and wife had been born at Dilhorne although the rest came from close by in the County. It was not uncommon to find an age difference of up to ten years between married couples although there were exceptions. Thomas Bolton of Godley Brook was a 61-year-old labourer who had been born in Dilhorne. In 1881 he was living with his wife who was 38 years younger (age 23) and their one-year-old son Daniel. William Flower, a sixty-nine year-old labourer, was living with his forty-seven year-old wife Emma and their two young children at Boundary.

Once people had settled here Dilhorne appeared to offer stability as, with only a few exceptions, all children were born in the parish, rather than married couples moving from place to place.

The Hall in 1881 was home to the Manningham Buller family and their staff. The hall itself was occupied by twenty-seven individuals, eight of who were family members, and a further three in the Lodge. The head of the household was Sir Edward, now aged eighty and a widower. The Hall was also home to Sir Edward's son Morton and his wife Mary, along with their three daughters Evelyn, Adelaide and Lillian. From their birthplaces it would appear that the family had previously lived at both Grosvenor Street and Eccleston Street in London, as well as at Trentham. Also resident at the Hall were two of Sir Edward's bachelor sons, Reginald and Frederick, captains in the Grenadier and Coldstream Guards respectively. Because the census is simply a snapshot of time the Hall may not have been the permanent home of these two individuals, especially when taking into account their professions.

Of the nineteen non-family members 15 were classed as domestic staff. The other four included a twenty-four year-old private governess, presumably employed for the three daughters of Morton, aged eleven, nine and seven, an agent, a soldier, and a soldier servant to Captain Buller. The fifteen individuals that composed the domestic staff included a cook who also acted as housekeeper. The male members of staff were the butler, three footmen and a groom. The remaining nine female servants included two housemaids, a lady's maid, nurse, nursery-maid, laundry-maid, kitchen-maid and scullery-maid. The majority were in their twenties and unmarried with the exception of a widow. Only two of the fifteen domestic servants had been born in Dilhorne, and another from nearby Kingsley. The remainder were from all areas of the country including Derbyshire, Birmingham, Gloucestershire, Hereford, Norfolk, Suffolk, Surrey, Middlesex, Devon, Cornwall and one individual from France. However, the opposite was true of the Lodge. This was the home of the coachman, Dilhorne-born Samuel Meskery, and his wife and daughter.

It is a misconception that during the past people did not live as long as today. Nine percent of the population of Dilhorne were aged sixty or over, with thirty-eight in their sixties, twenty-three in their seventies and seven octogenarians. The eldest was farmer Joseph Loton of The Croft, along with his seventy-seven year old wife and three adult children. Almost all of those aged sixty and over lived with kin, either adult unmarried children who were still at home, or occasionally adult grandchildren. A few had married offspring living with them but more commonly they would move into the homes of their married offspring to form part of their families. This was especially true of those who were widows or widowers, or the unmarried, who occasionally lived with a brother or sister.

Two unmarried individuals had no family with them. Retired clergyman John Chell, employed a housekeeper and a domestic servant rather than live on his own. Joseph Corbishley, a seventy year-old widower at Dilhorne Hall Farm on Godley Lane also employed a housekeeper along with four servants to assist with running the 133 acre farm. Only Mary Dunn of Park Hall, a sixty-one year old widow, lived on her own.

The most numerous occurrence of surnames studying the heads of households was that of Salt (13). This was followed by Harvey (8), Hurst and Thorley (both 6), Shoebotham (4) and Bettany, Bolton, Chell, Corbishley, Heath, Whitehurst, Wood and Wright (each 3). Three Salt families had settled in Godley Brook, including Joseph who was innkeeper at the Rose and Crown, in 1881. Herbert Salt kept the Royal Oak and was one of four Salt families living around the public house. At this time three of the Salts were publicans as another Joseph Salt was innkeeper of the Red Lion at Boundary.

That Godley brook was thought of as being separate from Dilhorne can be seen from the census return of Daniel Salt. Born in Dilhorne, but now living in Godley Brook, the first of his seven children were all recorded as being born in Dilhorne, while the latter three were stated as Godley Brook.[126]

Although there were a number of larger than average dwellings in Dilhorne some were less substantial. Those of the agricultural labourer or the miner would have consisted of a front room with kitchen scullery and two bedrooms above, and were dark and cramped by modern standards and with little or no sanitation. Some dwellings would have a rainwater tub but this would not be suitable for drinking. Instead water would have been carried from the nearest available source, either stream or well.

The interiors of these dwellings had changed little from that of their 17th century forefathers. Chairs would either flank the table and possibly an armchair and a settee might have been arranged around the fireplace. A dresser displayed the pans, pots and earthenware and china that the occupier possessed. Water would be heated in pans or kettles over the fire. Most households possessed a large zinc tub which would have been used for the weekly bath as well as for the washing of clothes. The bare floorboards may have appeared more cheerful with a handmade rug.

The fireplace being the focal point would have a mantelpiece of china ornaments and framed photographs of family members. A few may have had a built-in oven for baking bread. A print or two may have decorated the walls probably of a religious theme. On another wall hung the mirror. The tiny bedrooms above would have had most of their space taken up with the beds. For larger families this usually resulted in a tight squeeze. For an unlucky few bed would consist of rags and blankets on the floor in the corner of the room.

Bread and butter, or sometimes dripping, was the staple diet, along with oatcakes and porridge made from locally grown oats. Cheese was plentiful, along with pork, bacon, chicken, potatoes, cabbages and other green vegetables from garden or allotment. Weak tea was now a common drink for most although beer was still a popular choice along with homemade wines such as elderberry. The more industrious wives would have made jams and other preserves from what was available.

Footnotes

119. Pitt, William, p231 .
120. White's Directory of Staffordshire, 1851, p772-773.
121. Excludes Dilhorne Hall.
122. The enumerators for the 1881 census were Henry Carnwell, James Bagnall and Albert Edward Thorley.
123. 'Church Dilhorne' was also known as 'Church End.' A few of the older residents still remember this name being used. Another name this area was known by was 'Peg End' because of the card games played in the Colliers Arms in which a peg board and matches was used to keep score.
124. This figure includes both occupied and unoccupied dwellings but excludes the chapels and the church.
125. The sixteen servants at Dilhorne Hall were excluded from this figure so as not to bias the results.
126. A number of headstones in All Saints churchyard also evidence this.

15. Religious Affiliation

The great majority of parishioners of Dilhorne during the middle of the 17th century were Anglican, with only eleven non-conformists and two papists. Almost a hundred years later the figure for papists had increased to twenty-two.[127] This was not dissimilar to Cheadle with eighteen, although Draycott possessed 156. This extremely high figure was no doubt influenced by the staunch Catholic landowners, the Draycott family of Painsley Hall.

During the 19th century it became law to register any place intended for the use of public worship. In the middle of the 17th century non-conformists accounted for only 2% of the population nationally.[128] By 1851 this figure had risen to almost half of the population, and with a huge rise in the population. The steepest rise in non-conformity occurred during the second quarter of the 19th century, largely in the working classes. By 1813 a house at Dilhorne was registered for protestant dissenters by William Sargant, and another at Whitehurst by Richard Whitehurst.[129] Later Wesleyan chapels were built at Godley Brook[130] and Boundary.[131]

The 1851 Religious Census was undertaken by central government due to increased anxiety about church attendance, especially with the growth of dissenting religions and the restoration of the Roman Catholic hierarchy the previous year. Since the Act of Toleration in 1689 church attendance had no longer been compulsory and congregations had subsequently decreased. Each place of worship was assessed, and each denomination would have wished for higher figures, especially the Church of England who felt that they were losing their influence upon society. This is demonstrated by the varying comments which read like excuses as the numbers on the day the census was taken did not equal those of the average attendance during the preceding months

Church		Average number of attendants in the months preceding March 30th 1851			Estimated number attending Divine service on March 30th 1851		
		Morning	Afternoon	Evening	Morning	Afternoon	Evening
All Saints, Dilhorne (C of E)	General	125	95		75	60	
	School	85	80		80	71	
	Total	210	175		155	131	
St Peter's, Forsbrook (C of E)	General	220	200			95	
	School	50	30			25	
	Total	270	230			130	
Wesleyan Chapel, Boundary	General					28	29
	School					22	4
	Total					51	33
Wesleyan Chapel, Dilhorne	General					25	
	School					22	
	Total					47	

Table 10. The 1851 Religious Census

The figures were segregated into the general congregation and those attending Sunday school, with the combined total beneath these. During this period Sunday school was not exclusively for children. It is impossible to determine whether any of the 95 that attended the afternoon service at All Saints had also been part of the 125 that had attended the morning service.

The Reverend Boucher noted at Dilhorne that 'It was very wet and stormy - it was mid-lent Sunday, a day kept as a feast day in Staffordshire and the Squire of the parish with all his family and servants were away from home'. Boucher also completed the return for Forsbrook claiming 'This was the smallest congregation since the church was first opened. The fact that it was mid-Lent Sunday, a day of feasting in Staffordshire together with the very stormy weather of the day and the presence of influenza perhaps may account for it.' Francis Leigh, the curate of neighbouring Caverswall, blamed his lower than hoped for figures on the inconvenient position of the church in the south-east extremity of the parish and the recent erection of three new places of worship in adjoining parishes nearby. At Draycott Charles Stocker commented that the majority of parishioners were Roman Catholic, although the Catholic priest also commented 'the day being wet these numbers do not represent the average attendance.'

Footnotes

127. Worral, E S (ed.), 'Returns of Papists 1767. Vol.2' in 'Catholic Record Society Occasional Publications no.2, 1989).
128. Compton Census 1676.
129. Donaldson, Barbara (ed.), 'The Registrations of Dissenting Chapels and Meeting Houses in Staffordshire' in SHC, 4th series, vol.3.
130. Godley Brook Methodist Chapel is first mentioned in White's Directory of Staffordshire, 1851, p772-773.
131. The date 1827 is incorporated into the building.

The Wesleyan chapel at Godley Brook.

Godley Lane. The group of buildings on the left-hand side of the road include the former Rose and Crown public house - the first building.

The village school.

16. Education

Before the advent of schools any education was usually taught once a week by the village priest. The only education deemed necessary for the majority of people was a trade or skill with which they could earn a living in adulthood. The first school in Dilhorne is often rumoured to have been founded by the Earl of Huntingdon in the reign of Henry VIII. The Huntingdon family formerly held property in the parish through marriage to one of the co-heiresses of Sir John Port and did appear to hold patronage of the school.[132] However, this information appears to come from one person. John Holliday had written to the Earl at his Donnington Park home enquiring after any information about the origin of the school. In a reply from the Earl's steward, Mr E. Dawson, dated 20th June 1786, Dawson claimed the deeds could not be found but there were extracts copied from the originals. Further communication must have occurred, for by the mid-19th century a parishioner had what was supposed to be an extract of one of the deeds and certified by E. Dawson as having been compared with the original deed on the 27th September 1800.

The Marquis of Hastings succeeded to the property of the Earls of Huntingdon at Donnington, and like the Huntingdons, continued to exercise patronage of the school. However by this time, with the exception of an old plan of the estates belonging to the school, no other deeds or documents had survived. The belief that the school was founded by the Earls of Huntingdon rests solely upon Dawson's copy letter of 1800.[133]

It appears more likely that the school was founded by a vicar of Dilhorne, the Rev. John Whitacres in 1532, along with other parishioners. This was the believed version by those in the parish during the 17th century when a successor of Whitacres, the Rev. Richard Coke and five others stated the fact.[134] The substance of Dawson's letter is that the Earls of Huntingdon did grant the leases of the estates, although they were not responsible for the building of the school.

Copies of two deeds exist, dated 20th July 1559, granting rents to support a school and schoolmaster at Dilhorne. The deeds state a feoffment of twenty shillings rent from a messuage in Forsbrook occupied by William Morrys to support the schoolmaster. A further ten shillings rent came from a messuage in Cowneslowe for the maintenance of a free school for boys in the building lately built near the parish church.[135]

An illustration of this two-storied building appears in a sepia drawing from 184[136] To the left of the front doorway are two three-mullioned windows and another to the right. The presence of a second floor is indicated by a dormer window directly above the door, as well as on the gable end at the same level. The rear of the building is also visible in a watercolour of the rebuilt church of 1819.[137] A school for girls was established during the early 19th century by the widow of John Holliday, Lady Buller, and a Mrs Willatt, all of who resided at Dilhorne Hall during the second decade of the 19th century[138] although its location is unknown.

The original school was replaced in 1837 when the Marquis of Hastings erected another immediately to the left of the church.[139] This was used as a boys church school until 1876 when the present school was built for both boys and girls.

The majority of those aged between four and thirteen on the 1881 census were listed as scholars. It was unusual for those younger to be recorded although one three year-old girl who had an elder brother and sister may have gone to school because nobody else was at home; perhaps the mother was employed away from the house. One seven year-old was not listed as a scholar, possibly staying at home to look after her one year-old sister, her parents perhaps again at work.

Early 20th century at Dilhorne school.

Schoolchildren during the early 20th century.
Photo courtesy of Aubrey Salt.

Dilhorne school children c.1910.
Photo courtesy of Mick Faulkner.

Dilhorne school children in 1948.
Photo courtesy of Mick Faulkner.

Elementary education was made compulsory by the Education Acts of 1876 and 1880. Although no doubt hugely beneficial, this had an immediate effect upon the income of some families. Previously, and in particular in agricultural households, children contributed labour which would have been reduced when they entered into education. Some may have had casual or part-time work. With Dilhorne being largely agrarian children may have been employed on farms leading horses, bird-scattering, weeding, and in late summer harvest work. The school log book at neighbouring Caverswall records that the school was closed at the end of August 1869 to allow pupils to assist with the harvest.[140]

At least the children from Dilhorne did not have far to travel to school, with the exception of those from the outlying farmsteads such as Overmoor, Summer Hill and Heywood Grange. During summer berries would probably have been picked from the hedgerows on the way to school. In winter a child might have taken a potato that had sat in the ashes of the fire all night to keep their hands warm during the walk and to serve as a hot breakfast.

The interior of the classroom would have been neat rows of wooden desks with a blackboard behind the teachers desk at the front. Printed maps may have decorated the walls. It was in this room that the young of Dilhorne would learn the three Rs - reading, writing and arithmetic, along with religious education. Girls may also have been taught sewing and knitting. Older children would also have been taught history and geography. The school day ended at 4 o'clock except during winter when the children left at 3.30 so as to be able to return home in the light.

Footnotes

132. Pitt, William, p231. The same Sir John Port that founded a school at Repton in Derbyshire.
133. Griffith, George, 'Free Schools and Endowments of Staffordshire', p529-530.
134. Griffith, George, p529-530. In addition there exists in the National Archives an Action by Rowland Amery, executor of John Whytacres of Christ Church, Norwich, dated 1551-1553, on a bond for the application of fifty marks for the foundation of the free school in Dilhorne. TNA C 1/1318/16-18
135. William Salt Library, Stafford, William Salt Library M63 Copies of two deeds granting rents for the support of a school and schoolmaster at Dilhorne, 1559.
136. Dilhorne Church and Grammar School, sepia drawin g by J. Buckler, 1847. This, however, omits a mullioned window on the ground floor of the same gable end. William Salt Library. SV-IV 16 (45/8041). The drawing forms one of a pair, the other illustration being of the church from the south-east and showing part of the rear of the school. SV-IV (45/8054).
137. Dilhorne Church, watercolour, anonymous [L.J. Wood], c1819-1899. William Salt Library. SV-IV 15b. (45/8040).
138. Pitt, William, p231.
139. Short, George W., p12. This is probably the current 'Church House.'
140. Rogers, 'The Spirit of the Place', 2nd edition, p251.

The entrance to the boiler house under the tower. This brick-lined tunnel incorporates a Tudor-style stone doorway which may have originally been part of the school that abutted the churchyard.

17. Commerce

**This image from the early 20th century shows the Royal Oak on the left
with the three cottages that used to adjoin the public house.**
Photo courtesy of Aubrey Salt.

Before the 19th century most provisions would have been purchased from Cheadle or another of the nearby towns. The majority of 17th and 18th century wills simply state gentleman, yeoman or husbandmen, along with occasional specific trades such as miner. With the exception of a blacksmith and a shoemaker, none record what may be thought of as supplying provisions for the community. However, one commodity that was provided on a commercial basis was drink.

Alehouses were the forerunners of public houses. They had existed since the medieval period and had slowly contributed to the decline of the church. Previously the church and churchyard had been a venue for social gatherings such as games, plays, celebrations, the bartering of surplus goods and a place for village business to be conducted. Long before the 18th century these activities had gradually shifted to the alehouse. After the church had performed the perfunctory service associated with baptisms, marriages and burials the assembled would reconvene to the alehouse to celebrate the event.

Alehouses offered the community a convenient and usually warm and hospitable meeting place. Externally it would have appeared similar to many of the other dwellings, a room furnished with tables and benches where customers could relax by the fireside, enjoy a game of cards or dice, and exchange news and gossip away from the scrutiny of the local incumbent. There may have been a meagre fayre on offer such as bread and cheese or pies but little else. It was due to this that they were considered inferior to inns and taverns that, in addition to ale, also sold wines and spirits, provided warm meals and could offer accommodation for both man and horse.

Keeping an alehouse was relatively straightforward and required little capital outlay although it did necessitate obtaining a license from the Justice of the Peace. Some were short-lived ventures operating from an ordinary dwelling in the community. Although the majority of licenses were issued to males they were usually run by the wife of the household who would both brew the ale and serve the customers, hence the term alewife. The husband probably had a different occupation so that the profit from running the alehouse would have been an additional form of income. Some husbands may have run them as an alternative to unemployment. Although the names of the alehouses are omitted the following table shows those who applied for such licenses at the end of the 18th century.

	1782	1783	1784	1785	1786	1787	1788	1789	1790	1791	1792
Nehemiah Banks	X		X	X	X					X	X
Mary Martin (Forsbrook)	X	X	X	X				X	X	X	X
Seth Rigby (Forsbrook)	X	X	X	X	X	X	X	X			
Anthony Warrillow	X	X	X	X	X	X	X	X	X	X	X
Catherine Moss		X	X	X	X		X	X	X	X	X
George Martin (Blythe Br)		X				X	X	X	X	X	
Elizabeth Ratcliffe		X	X	X	X	X					
William Thorley		X	X	X	X	X	X	X	X	X	X
Richard Phillips				X	X						
William Banks (Forsbrook)						X	X	X	X		
John Griffin						X	X	X	X	X	X
Thomas Wilshaw							X				
Joseph Chell								X	X	X	
Joseph Warrillow (Forsbrook)									X	X	X

Table 11. Register of Persons Licensed to Keep Alehouses 1782-1792.[141]

The table shows a total of fourteen names for the eleven-year period. Four individuals were listed as being in Forsbrook and one in Blythe Bridge. That suggests that a total of nine alehouses were in operation in Dilhorne and Boundary at the end of the 18th century. There is no way of knowing whether the alehouse kept by Seth Rigby at Forsbrook, who last applied for a license in 1789, was that taken over by Joseph Warrillow from 1790. The recurrences of surnames, along with the corresponding dates, may suggest that William Banks temporarily took over the running of Nehemiah's alehouse. Similarly both Anthony and Joseph Warrillow, and George and Mary Martin may also have been related.

The vestry took a keen interest in regards to their parishioners and the subject of drink. In 1798 they resolved that 'complaint will be duly made to the magistrates not to grant licenses to any publican in the townships of Dilhorne and Forsbrook who shall neglect to shut up their houses and send their company home to their families at or before the hour of 10 o'clock in the evening, or who shall not put up and observe the printed rules and orders distributed by order of the quarter sessions or from proper authority relating to the good government of alehouses.'

The fact that the first of the nine signatures approving this was that of John Holliday, the local Justice of the Peace, possibly meant that this order would have been ardently employed. However, not everyone appears to have complied. On Monday December 30th 1805 Thomas Thorley and Mary Hurst, both of Dilhorne, reported to Edward Powys, a Justice of the Peace, that on the previous Sunday publican Anne Lowe had allowed 'drinking and tippling within her house' and was ordered to forfeit the sum of 10s.[142]

The Hollybush may have been the oldest public house in the district. It was first mentioned in 1800 when Robert Parker, the Lord of the Manor, called a Court Baron and Court Survey on September 25th 'at the house of John Loton known by the sign of the Hollybush'[143] It may also have been the venue where Justices of the Peace convened to conduct their business when in the district. It ceased trading before the end of the 19th century and the large three-storied building still exists opposite the Royal Oak at the bottom of the Common. A reminder of its days as a public house can still be seen on the ground outside the frontage where barrels were rolled down into the cellar beneath.[144]

By the 1830s there was a grocer and currier, a corn miller and shopkeeper, a maltster, a blacksmith and five butchers. The village now had three public houses - the Hollybush (Joseph Loton), the Colliers Arms (Joseph Phillips) and the Royal Oak (Thomas Thorley). This, like the Hollybush, was also a meeting place for conducting local business, such as the auction that was held there of four new dwellings at Godley Brook in 1857.[145] In addition to these were two beer houses, one run by Emanuel Whitehurst and the other by John Carnwell of Godley Brook.[146] These were a result of the Beer Act of 1830, introduced to encourage the drinking of a native product, as opposed to public houses that could now sell both wines and spirits. Like alehouses, they could be established for a relatively modest fee compared to a public house licence, many simply using the front room of a house.

By 1851 commerce consisted of a single butcher, a grocer and draper, a miller and shopkeeper, a maltster, a tailor, a blacksmith, two wheelwrights and three boot and shoemakers. The three public houses were still in existence - the Colliers Arms (Mary Rigby), the Royal Oak (Joseph Salt) and the Hollybush (Joseph Loton). The number of beer houses had also increased to three, run by Edwin James, George James and Henry Slater.[147]

By 1896 the Post Office was in operation opposite the toll house.[148] This also functioned as a grocers, tailors and drapers. There were two butchers, two blacksmiths, a wheelwright and a tea dealer at Godley Lane.[149] Only the Colliers Arms (Samuel Maskery) and the Royal Oak (John Shelley) were mentioned by name. Joseph Salt, who had previously been licensee of the

Royal Oak, was now a beer retailer at Godley Brook and William Shingler and Mrs Margaret Salt were both beer retailers at Boundary. Law and order was controlled by police constable, George Pitcher.[150]

The Wakes were an ancient festival most popular towards the end of the 19th century and celebrated on November 1st, All Saints Day. It was a day when some of the church charity money was distributed amongst the poor of the parish. The day began with a church service, followed by neighbours exchanging dishes of furmety (traditionally made from hulled wheat with milk and raisins) with apples handed out to the children. A tea party was held at the school between four and five in the afternoon when parishioners gathered at tables laden with sandwiches and cakes, and presided over by Mrs Fielden. There were so many attending that this necessitated two sittings. In the evening a concert of singers and the choir was held, along with a dance in the school hall.

In 1899 a group of village notables formed a branch of the Ancient Order of Foresters, a branch of which was already flourishing in Cheadle. The Dilhorne branch was known as the Court Excelsior. They were a benevolent society to which members paid a weekly subscription. Payments were made for loss of earnings during illness as well as financial assistance during times of family bereavement. The society celebrated its foundation each year in June with a procession known as Club Day, headed by the Foresters on horseback. They were followed by a richly-coloured banner and a uniformed band. The community gathered near Godley Brook and marched to the school where a brief stop was made for light lunch.

Afterwards they continued to the church where a short service was held by the honorary chaplain of the order, the Reverend George Plant. They continued to the vicarage lawn (now part of Tithe Barn Cottage garden) where the children enjoyed sticky buns and a glass of milk. Later in the afternoon a roast beef dinner was held at the Royal Oak for the principal members and guests. The remainder of the day was spent enjoying a fun fair in the Royal Oak field including donkey rides, swing boats a helter-skelter, and various sports with prizes for the winners.

Footnotes

141. Staffordshire Record Office. Q/RLv/1.
142. Staffordshire Record Office. Q/SB 1805 a 35.
143. Manorial Survey, 25th September 1800. This document confirms that by this time the manor was composed of a larger number of small estates.
144. Apparently the cellar still contains the shelves around the walls where the barrels were stored.
145. Staffordshire Record Office. D5226/30.
146. White's Directory of Staffordshire, 1834, p743. Interestingly The Red Lion at Boundary was omitted.
147. White's Directory of Staffordshire, 1851, p772-773. Again The Red Lion at Boundary was not listed.
148. At one point this also functioned as the Police House.
149. John Salt.
150. Kelly's Directory of Staffordshire, 1896, p140.

Club Day, early 20th century, showing the procession including the village band at the beginning of New Road. Photo courtesy of Aubrey Salt.

Club Day early 20th century, showing Ancient Order of Foresters outside the Royal Oak.
Photo courtesy of Aubrey Salt.

**Club Day, 1915, showing a group of children
assembled on the vicarage lawn.**

Club Day, 1915, showing a group of children marching towards Blakeley Bank.
Photo courtesy of Aubrey Salt.

The village band with bandleader Mr I J Smith in the centre front, early 20th century.
Photo courtesy of Mick Faulkner.

**The former public house, The Hollybush. It was here in the late 18th
and early 19th centuries that the manorial court conducted its business.**

The Royal Oak, a modern photo with the cottages now demolished and a car park in place.

A horse and cart makes its slow way towards the Village stores.
Photo courtesy of Mick Faulkner.

The Royal Oak on the right showing two of the three cottages that used to adjoin the public house. The gate leads to the gardens of Dilhorne Hall. Photo courtesy of Mick Faulkner.

Village stores and post office on the left and the police house on the right.
Photo courtesy of Mick Faulkner.

**The village bandleader, Mr I J Smith of
Rock Cottage, early 20th century.**
Photo courtesy of Mick Faulkner.

BELOW:
**Club Day and the Foresters banner outside
the Colliers Arms (later Charlie Bassett's
and now White Lion).**
Photo courtesy of Mick Faulkner.

18. The Twentieth Century

One of the most gruesome murders in North Staffordshire during the 20th century was that involving a husband and wife at their New Close Fields farmhouse on Sunday September 27th 1903. The following Saturday on October 3rd the *Staffordshire Advertiser* reported the shocking tragedy in detail. John Brundred had been born in Cauldon, the son of George Brundred, publican of the Yew Tree Inn. He had been married for about twenty years and had lived happily with his wife Sarah Ann and their three children. He had worked at Park Hall Colliery for about twenty-five years and had gained the confidence of the miners placed under his care by his careful conduct of the engine. A few weeks before the incident he had injured his leg while working at the conductors in the pit. Despite the injury he continued working but after a few weeks medical advice was summoned and he was ordered home.

His detention at home appeared to make him despondent, having previously enjoyed the best of health, and his fellow workmen who visited him at intervals advised him to pull himself together and not to give up. Early on Sunday September 27th he was visited by relatives and friends who noticed a marked change to his demeanour, with Brundred complaining that he should never recover and that more would be heard of it later. A medical practitioner was called and advised his removal to the asylum at Cheddleton but his wife pleaded that he should remain at home.

About 6pm screams were heard coming from the house, and neighbours from an adjoining farm rushed to the house where they saw seventeen year-old Ernest Brundred who said that his mother was dead and that his father was cutting her with a knife. On entering the house they were confronted with a shocking scene. Brundred's wife Sarah Ann was lying face downwards with her head almost severed from her body. Brundred was kneeling on her back, and it appeared as if he was bumping her head on the floor, which was covered in blood. The horrified witnesses tried to pull him off the body, but Brundred, who was a powerfully-built man, resisted their efforts and then turned on the neighbours who fled in fear.

Summoning the local policeman, Constable Stanley, they returned to the farmhouse and through the window they saw Brundred lying on the hearth with a large wound in his throat and a razor by his side. At that point Brundred was still alive, but only barely, and died shortly afterwards. During the initial attack Sarah Ann must have frantically struggled in terror as her hands were fearfully cut and her throat was cut from right to left, the head being nearly severed from her body. A regrettable feature of the tragedy was that the little daughter of the unfortunate couple, besides her elder brother, witnessed the occurrence.

An enquiry into the event took place in the church rooms, probably Church House, at Dilhorne on Tuesday evening in the presence of the coroner Mr C. T. Cull. The first witness was the eldest son, Ernest, a teacher at a Wesleyan Day School. He stated that he thought his father had been acting peculiar for about a week. At the time of the incident he had been in a nearby meadow with a friend when he heard his mothers screams. He rushed into the house and called to the friend to get help. When he got inside he saw his mother on the floor with his father on top of her. He tried to pull his father away but was unable to do so.

His father had always been kind to him and his mother. He added that his father had never threatened them before although several times recently had remarked that 'nothing had happened in the annals of history like what was going to happen.' Other witnesses gave similar statements reciting the same. The conclusion was that Brundred had suffered a fit of insanity during which he took the life of his wife and then his own. Both were aged forty-three. The funeral took place the following afternoon at Cheadle Cemetery. Two hearses chauffeured the two coffins and the path was lined with mourners from Church Terrace to the cemetery chapel, including a large number of employees from Park Hall Colliery.

During the first decade of the 20th century there was a shopkeeper, a butcher, a blacksmith, a carpenter and a brickmaker. The Licensees of the Colliers Arms (Joseph Wright Radford) and the Royal Oak (John Shelley) were also practicing farmers, and Joseph Salt was still classed as a beer retailer at Godley Brook.[151]

By 1912 the only traders operating in the village beside the greengrocer was a joiner and a blacksmith. The Colliers Arms and the Royal Oak still had the same occupiers as six years before, and were augmented by Edward Bentley a beer retailer.[152]

The Holly Bush had ceased trading as a public house before the end of the 19th century. During the early years of the 20th century the front room was used as a fruit shop by the Parr family, while the large room at the rear was used by the village band for practice sessions following its formation in 1912. The band was formed by Mr I J Smith of Rock Cottage, who was the estate manager for the Hall, and who had played with other bands in Burton and Leicestershire before coming to Dilhorne in 1909. He decided in October 1912 to form a village band. He rented thirty instruments from a Company in Birmingham and recruited twenty-four of the village men, only three of whom knew a note of music. By June the following year they were considered proficient enough to lead the Club Day parade. A fund was begun to buy uniforms which had been acquired by 1914.

During the First World War the band often joined forces with the Forsbrook band because so many members had been called up. On Christmas mornings at seven o'clock they used to play carols and hymns outside the village shop including *Christians Awake* and *Salute This Happy Morning*. The band continued into the 1920s but dissolved when Mr Smith left the community and nobody could be found to take over the role of bandleader.

In Rose Cottage, next to the shop, lived Mr Thornton, coachman at the Hall. When he moved to Clematis Cottage in 1915 it was then tenanted by William Boulton, the blacksmith and wheelwright, along with his apprentice Herbert Key. His smithy was at the rear of Holly Bush House, being a group of large buildings that included the former stables from when the house had been an inn. The smithy was worked well into the 1920s which included the shoeing of pit ponies belonging to Foxfield Colliery.

Opposite Rock Cottage were the old Grammar School houses built during the 18th century. They housed the schools usher as well as boarding some of the pupils. In the first house at the beginning of the 20th century lived the Faulkner family. Richard Faulkner had been groom at the Hall for two decades. At the beginning of the First World War he joined the Derbyshire Yeomanry but was invalided home suffering from a haemorrhage of the lung in February 1915. He died on February 27th leaving a wife, a son Edward and daughter Nancy (later Salt). Faulkner had been one of the 118 men from the parish that enlisted during the First World War, including Major Fielden and his son William, who was badly injured in a campaign in Gallipoli in 1915 and returned home. Next to the Faulkners lived Joseph Wright who for many years was sexton at the church.

The end of the War saw great changes both economically and socially, and this resulted in the Dilhorne Estate being offered for auction in September 1919 (the remainder was auctioned in 1943). Many of the tenants took advantage to purchase their properties. There were fifty lots covering 494 acres of land including farms, cottages, pubs, the shop and the police house. The largest farms were Callowhill (50 acres), Day House Farm and Cresswell Ford Farm (both 41 acres), and Old Whitehurst Farm (29 acres), as well as numerous smallholdings including Blakeley House, Whitehurst Farm, and cottages in Sarver Lane, Godley Barn, Madgedale, and eighteen acres of land adjoining the school.

As previously detailed, the Fieldens left the Hall in 1923. This was offered for sale but failing to attract interest was finally demolished four years later. Legend claims that a tunnel runs from Dilhorne Hall to Stansmoor. The entrance to this was supposedly located behind the wall where the present Village Hall stands, and came up somewhere near the front wall close to the road. The tunnel runs under the bowling green, not far below the surface as on one occasion those playing bowls heard the voices of children from under the pitch. Shortly after this incident the entrance was bricked up.[153]

By the 20th century Park Hall Colliery was owned by William Eli Bowers of Caverswall Castle. Upon his death in 1911 his son William Aubrey Bowers took over the management of the business. At the beginning of the First World War thirty-five men enlisted in the armed forces, four of who lost their lives including Bowers. In 1919 a memorial was erected at the colliery but when this was acquired by the Foxfield Colliery during the late 1920s the monument was also transferred. The front of the memorial records the names of the four who were killed.

Lieut W. A. Bowers of the North Staffs Regt. Died of wounds 2nd July 1916.

Pte C. A. Hughes of the East Lancs Regt. Died in action 1st August 1918

Pte K. Lovatt of the Northumberland Fusiliers. Died in Germany 5th Dec 1918

Pte L. E. Nutt of the Suffolk Regt. Killed in action 2nd Oct 1918

The reverse lists the thirty-one others who served and returned.

By the end of the 1920s the Colliers Arms and the Royal Oak were in the respective tenancies of Joseph Beardmore and William Thomas Hatton. Supplementing these was a beer house at Godley Brook maintained by William Sales. Enoch Dale was both postmaster and shopkeeper, and Rupert Oakley of Church Farm was a milk seller.[154]

Enoch Dale and his wife Margaret took over running the village shop during the First World War, taking over the business from Margaret's parents who had operated it from the beginning of the 20th century. Enoch and Margaret ran the shop for over fifty years before their son Francis and his wife Vera took over the business in 1967. Margaret later recalled that 'during the War when the law required bread to be at least twelve hours old before it could be sold we would be up until after midnight baking it.'[155]

The interior with its large wooden counters consisted of the shop on one side and the Post Office on the other. This continued to operate into the 21st century. During the early to mid 20th century there was also a small general stores at Boundary.

Although the shop catered for all the community's needs during the 1920s, fresh vegetables and greenhouse produce could also be purchased from the gardener at Dilhorne Hall, Mr Makepeace, as well as his successor Mr Johnson, at the gardener's house accessed through a gate in the Hall garden wall.

During the 1930s William Blood had taken over the running of the Royal Oak[156] and by 1940 George Townsend was the licensee of the Rose and Crown at Godley Brook.[157]

During the first half of the 20th century a cricket ground existed by the old pools. This was provided by Major Fielden and had a pavilion and scoreboard. The club was headed by Sir William Fielden, the Reverend George Plant, Mr Deveraux and Mr Mear of Dilhorne House. The annual celebration of the formation of the team was held every Shrove Tuesday at the Royal Oak.

The Grand Cricket Match of 1913 was a competition of the men's team against the women's team. As women were regarded as being the weaker sex it was agreed that the men should be handicapped. Therefore the men were only allowed to bat with one hand, the other remaining behind their back. The men, even with this handicap, still managed to win the match, after which both sides were invited to take tea with Lady Fielden at the Hall.

By the 1950s the club had moved to the Common. This ground, like its predecessor, had its own pavilion, with Sundays regarded as Cricket Day and very much a family affair. Along with cricket and football the children in Dilhorne during the early 20th century would also frequent the bathing pool by the old boating lake.

The Second World War had little physical effect upon the community. During hostilities a stack of nine bombs fell in the fields near to the fishponds. This was as a result of a chink of light showing from a nearby house seen by planes aiming for the factory at Froghall. The most interest was that of the children that would go down to the site to collect shrapnel as souvenirs, which may have included the seven or eight evacuees from Manchester that were billeted in the community during the War.

During the early hours of 30th January 1943 a Vickers Wellington from the Operational Training Unit at R.A.F Wymeswold near Loughborough crashed at Dilhorne during a practice exercise. At 2.15am the plane flew into the ground in low cloud killing two of the five crew members. A small memorial still marks the place. The following year, almost to the day, history appeared to repeat itself. On January 31st 1944 an Armstrong Whitworth Whitley from Whitchurch Heath in Shropshire, also on a training exercise, crashed near Hardiwick at the eastern edge of the parish. Of the five-man crew only one member survived.

In 1953 yet another air tragedy occurred near Dilhorne. On March 27th an English Electric Canberra with a three-man crew was carrying out a training exercise from R.A.F. Scampton near Lincoln. The plane was almost vertical upon impact and the three men died instantly. Due to the level of destruction the R.A.F. court was unable to decide whether the cause of the accident was mechanical or human error.

Before Severn Trent supplied mains water to the community it came from springs and a collection of tanks in Stansmoor Wood, with pipes laid from there to a reservoir near to the fishponds. From there it reached the village partly by gravitation and by hydraulic pumps with the pump house located near to the rear entrance gates to Dilhorne Hall. Taps were installed for the inhabitants at the Royal Oak, the School House, Whympney, Godley Brook and Whitehurst.

The Colliers Arms was taken over by Ralph Charlie Bassett in 1947, having previously been a farmer and cattle transporter. The Bassett family lived at Blakeley House and Charlie's father had been gatekeeper for the Foxfield Colliery where the line crosses the road when coal was transported to the junction with the main line at Blythe Bridge. By 1970 the Rose and

Crown was in the hands of retired police officer Nathaniel George Shaw.

Thomas Chadwick became headmaster of the school in 1939, with his daughter Marjorie one of the teachers. He held the post for thirty-one years before being superseded by Dennis Darlington in 1970.[158] During the early 1970s Marjorie Chadwick remarked that 'Dilhorne has changed ...there was a time when I knew everyone in the village, but strangers come in and buy property and you lose touch.' Similarly, the Reverend Ernest Marsh noted that 'the village lies in a Green Belt area and because of the restrictions, it is slowly tending to kill off village life.'[159]

The Foxfield Light Railway Society was formed in 1967 after being given an old 1903 engine which had finished its life in a Welsh steel works. By 1973 the collection had increased to twelve engines, as well as one diesel, and it utilised the track from the old colliery to the sidings adjacent to the main line at Blythe Bridge.

Ceramic designer Susie Cooper lived at the Old Parsonage until emigrating to the Isle of Man in 1987. This had been the former home of Francis Wedgwood, a direct descendant of Josiah wedgwood and director of his ancestors business.

During the early 1980s the population of Dilhorne was 335 occupying a total of 141 dwellings, sixteen of which were council houses. Development during the 20th century included the council houses built shortly after the Second World War and the bungalows built during early 1970s in School Close to house the occupants of the row of three cottages that were demolished adjoining the Royal Oak. These bungalows had subsidised purchases for those already living in the community.

A few years after the bungalows further houses were built. A number of other properties were demolished during the mid-20th century due to subsidence. This included Carfax on Dilhorne Common which had formerly been a colliery manager's house. Table 12 shows how the figures compared with neighbouring villages. Even combining the segregated figures of Dilhorne and Boundary the community was still considerably smaller than those that surrounded it.

	Population	No. of Dwellings	Council Houses
Dilhorne	335	125	16
Boundary	144	48	0
Forsbrook	1914	682	36
Caverswall & Cookshill	1066	357	0
Blythe Bridge	2019	769	235

Table 12. Population and Housing 1983[160]

Scrap-metal worker Eddie Heath has been building replicas of famous landmarks for Bonfire night since 1988. Housed on ground behind the Royal Oak these charity-raising events have included Wembley Stadium, the Houses of Parliament and Big Ben (1996), Dracula's Castle (1998), The Royal Oak (2004), The White House (2006) and The Tower of London (2008).

During the first week of May 2009, the BBC descended upon Dilhorne and the Foxfield Railway. These locations were to feature in the Christmas special of the period drama Cranford. The Village Hall was used as a base by both crew and the actors to change into their costumes. Filming took place both at Foxfield Colliery and the on the railway. This included changing one of the signs to Hanbury Holt. Cathie Davy, BBC publicist for the series, said that the location was chosen because the landscape of Dilhorne is perfect because 'we can get great panoramic shots of scenery without the trappings of modern-day life'.[161]

Footnotes

151. Kelly's Directory of Staffordshire, 1904, p153-154.
152. Kelly's Directory of Staffordshire, 1912, p166.
153. Much of this information has come from the oral testimonies of Aubrey Salt and Marcia Curl (nee Salt).
154. Kelly's Directory of Staffordshire, 1928, p178.
155. Staffordshire Weekly Sentinel, April 27th 1973, p6. Focus on Folk column 'Where The Iron Horse is Still Cherished.'
156. Kelly's Directory of Staffordshire, 1932, p174.
157. Kelly's Directory of Staffordshire, 1940, p172. About this time there was also a pub on the left-hand side of the lane leading up to the entrance to Foxfield Colliery, possibly called The Lamb.
158. Other staff included Mrs Patricia Mayers (teacher), Mrs Christine Gilman (assistant), Mrs Iris Hurst (secretary), and Miss Isobel Salt and Miss Daisy Salt (both kitchen assistants), and Mrs Dora Sales (caretaker). She took over the role from her mother in the early 1950s who had held the post for twenty years. By the 1970s meals were no longer prepared and cooked on the premises but were delivered from Cheadle.
159. Staffordshire Weekly Sentinel, April 27th 1973, p6. Focus on Folk column 'Where The Iron Horse is Still Cherished.'
160. Staffordshire Record Office. C/P/99. Community Council of Staffordshire. Village Facilities Survey compiled by Stanley H. Beaver, 24th Sept 1983.
161. The Sentinel newspaper, 3rd June 2009.

The lodge to Dilhorne Hall, now converted for domestic use. The original entrance ran through the central living space of the building.

George Shaw, Rose and Crown.

Charlie Bassett.

Two mid-20th century publicans

The village amateur dramatic society.
Photo courtesy of Aubrey Salt.

**The site of Dilhorne Hall showing the steps that once divided
the upper and lower front lawns. The Village Hall stands nowadays in the background.**

The Mothers Union during the 1940s with the
Rev. James Birch in the centre.

**Richard Faulkner in the stable grounds at
Dilhorne Hall. Richard was Sir William
Fielden's groom.** Courtesy of Mick Faulkner.

**Sir William Fielden outside the south
front of Dilhorne Hall. Both photos early 20thC.**
Courtesy of Mick Faulkner.

Dr Worrall presenting the Club Bowling Cup to Mick Faulkner late 1980s.

Champion smiles. Captain John Green and colleagues of the Dilhorne Bowling Club who won the trophy for the Division 3 league title and reached the semi-final of the Junior Cup 1990s.

Well bowled: Dilhorne Recreation Bowling Club C team with captain Barry Mawson and the cup for the Stoke on Trent League VIII title. Three newspaper cuttings courtesy of Mick Faulkner.

Chatfield House - Then. This early 20th century photo courtesy of Mick Faulkner.
Below - Now.

The clergy and choir during the 1950s. Back L-R John Wright, Billy Wright, Brian Salt, Ian Wright.
Third row Mick Faulkner, David Carrea, Eddie Faulkner, Alan Spendelow, Roy Salt, Ralph Basset,
Cecil Wainwright. Second row Mr Waterfield (organist), Alfred Stanley (vicar), Ken Burston.
Front row Jim Faulkner, Gordon Basset, Reg Spendlow, Clive Brassington.
Photo courtesy of Mick Faulkner.

Dilhorne in the early 20th century.
Photo courtesy of Mick Faulkner.

19. Memorials

A number of interesting memorials both within the church and churchyard exist for people from Dilhorne's past.

Anne Adderley is the 'divided' corpse. She was born in 1681, the daughter of Arden Adderley of Hames Hall in Warwickshire. She became the third wife of Samuel Adderley, born 1667, of Blakehall. He died in 1716 at the age of forty-nine leaving Anne a widow. She later married Caesar Colclough of Delph House and died in 1724 at the relatively young age of forty-three. She is buried inside the church, her memorial being next to Caesar Colclough, although her first husband's memorial also lays claim to her being interred near this place.

Certain inscriptions offer clues as to how a person died. The headstone of Thomas Heath of Forsbrook who died aged fifty-eight in 1805 reads:

> **Affliction fore [sic] long time bore - physicians were in vain**
> **till God did please to give me ease - and free me from my pain.**

A popular verse also found on a few other headstones in the churchyard.

A more specific description of the cause of death appears on the headstone of Ann, the wife of Nehemiah Banks, of Forsbrook, who died at the age of thirty in 1791:

> **The pains of childbirth over powered me**
> **I did submit to death with fights you see**
> **As my creator thought it best that I**
> **Should be in bliss and everlasting joy.**

The headstone also records *Also of two children issue of the above who died young* - a similar record is also found on other headstones.

There is always something melancholic about reading memorial inscriptions of those who died in childhood. Samuel and Jane Brassington lost seven children in the space of six years.

In memory of the four children issue of Samuel and Jane Brassington
of this parish of Caverswall who died as followeth

Prudence	February 17th 1776	1 month
Mary	June 28th 177?	1 year
Samuel	December 22nd 1775	2 years
Edward	December 29th 1775	7 months
Ann	April 25th 1778	15 years
Ellen	May 2nd 1781	6 years
Jane	July 7th 1781	4 years

An anomaly is that the headstone clearly states 'of this parish of Caverswall'. Possibly this is a reference to Samuel and Jane's parish of birth rather than that of their children. Perhaps after marriage the couple had migrated to Dilhorne where the children had been born which explains their interment in the churchyard.

The sudden death of seventeen year old Thomas Baker of Newclose Fields on 12th December 1811 is clear:

Dilhorne in the early 20th century.
Photo courtesy of Mick Faulkner.

By sudden death I'm snatched away
Death fiercely left me time to say
The Lord have mercy on my soul
So absolute is his control
Reflect when thou grave dost see
The next that's made may be for thee.

An unusual entry appears on the headstone of John Robey of Blaklee Lane who died in 1808 aged 76 and Catherine the wife of Sampson Wright of Captain Barn who died the same year aged 48. *'Also of Mary daughter of the above who died 12th March 1809 aged 20 years'*.

Here lies a damsel who alas
A false young man deceived
Handsome, as faithless, rover was
And she to death was grieved
Let faithless rover range
for she has fixed her heart on one
whose love can never change.

Who her suitor was is unknown but it is a clear case of pointing the finger. What exactly the cause of death was is also unknown. The entry in the parish register simply states Mary Wright from New Barn Caverswall parish interred March 16th.

The accidental death of a collier is recorded on the headstone of William George of Daisy Bank who died 28th February 1925 aged twenty. The inscription reads: *Erected by the officials and workmen of New Haden Colliery. Cheadle, as a token of respect.*

Some headstones record the worthiness of the individuals they commemorate such as Richard Whitehurst who died in 1841 aged eighty-two:

The rich since this good man resigned his breath
have lost a good example by his death
the poor have reason to lament his end
for every winter'll show they've lost a friend.

The inscription of John Shufflebotham of Bank Top who died in 1845 at the age of sixty-seven reads:

His life showed the advantages which industry, frugality and sobriety
confer after a severe and protracted illness which he endured with fortitude.
He expired in peace in the bosom of his family, through life he obtained
much respect, and his death was lamented by a large circle of friends.
This stone is erected as a monument of affectionate regard by his bereaved
widow and children on who deeply mourn the loss of a husband and father

THE MOTOR CAR COMES TO DILHORNE.

Courtesy of Mick Faulkner.

Conclusion

Attempting to write a historical narrative is similar to doing a jigsaw with many of the pieces missing. The story of Dilhorne has been written with only fragmentary evidence. Sadly no consistent run of 14th or 15th century manorial records survive. Neither does a 16th century rectors diary, a 17th century annotated pew plan, or the jottings of an 18th century farmer's wife. In many instances the bare bones of statistics have been used to paint a picture of these forefathers of the hamlet. Similarly, only brief snatches of lives appear in plea rolls, overseers accounts and other parochial documentation.

Similarly the community itself is like a jigsaw, with the hall, the village shop, the local pub, the school and church all distinct pieces. The introduction of county councils in 1888 meant a decline in power and influence of the gentry resulting in a loss of interest in their ancestral, and often rural, homes. The large pile that was Dilhorne Hall survived into the 20th century but now only the former lodge survives.

The combined village shop and post office has disappeared, no longer viable due to the high proportion of individuals with cars and the convenience of nearby supermarkets. However, in the larger picture the shop was only a short-lived venture of less than a century, when compared to the total community history. It answered the needs of the inhabitants and was a result of farmers no longer producing purely for subsistence, and a wider variety of foodstuffs through importation and mass-produced goods.

The police station too has gone with policing administered from centralised units. Two of the four public houses have ceased trading as publicans are no longer brewing their own product but simply acting as a provider. Although the community still has two public houses many people drink at home or in a local which may be a distance away, just as some who frequent the public houses in Dilhorne may come from outside the community.

Likewise children no longer receive their secondary education at the local school, instead travelling to larger schools in nearby towns. The parish, previously having an incumbent of its own, now shares one with other parishes, reflecting both a decline in importance and a dwindling congregation. The vestry and the overseers no longer administer village governance or parochial relief. Although never completely reliant upon its own resources, the community is now almost totally dependent upon those from outside.

The impact of industry in the form of mining contributed towards the building of prosperous houses, as well as providing employment. If it was not for this rural industrialisation it is likely that the population would have stagnated or fallen as a larger number of individuals would have emigrated in search of employment. Many did indeed still migrate, pushed because there was not enough employment or housing within the community, and pulled by the prospect of a steady wage through regular employment in the growing industries of the Potteries, rather than casual farm work.

Changes in farming practice greatly reduced the amount of labour required although it was still the largest employer of the community, producing for the ready markets of the expanding towns.

Appendix

Rectors and Vicars of Dilhorne (plaque within church)

	Rectors and Vicars	Patron
1166	Hugh persona de Dulverne	Ruold de Dulverne
1170	Robert de Coppenhale	Roger, Prior of Stone
1310	William de Kenilworth, rector	Dean and Chapter of Lichfield
1313	John de Codeshall, (ob 1319) vicar	ditto same to present.
1319	Robert de Caumpedene, rector	
1321	Edmund de Draycote, rector	
1406	Alexander Benet, vicar	
1509 1547	Sir Thomas Tomkynson*	
1535	John Wright, (ob 1573) vicar	
1573 1617	Richard Cook	
1617 1651	Thomas Cantrell	
1651 1656	William Thomson	
1660 1700	Thomas Dresser	
1700 1721	John Cope	
1721 1731	Edward Taylor	
1732	W. Budworth, (ob 1809) James Daniell	
1809	Henry White, (ob 1836)	
	New aisle rebuilt at a cost of £1,000	
1836 1863	Charles T. Dawes	
1863 1883	Jas. Harold Walker, vicar	
1883	John Beckett, (ob 1902) vicar	
1902	George Ralph Plant, M.A. (ob 1929).	
	Both he and his wife were devastated when their son was killed in a motorbike accident in 1927. George died in 1936 at the age of sixty-four.	
1929 1939	St. John Guy Maule Vernon, vicar to Kiddlington, Oxford	
1940 1949	James Taylor Birch, vicar to Tamworth	
1950 1957	Alfred Stanley, vicar to Tamworth	
1957 1964	George Edward Weaver, vicar to Sutton Coldfield	
1966 1969	Temporary priest in charge Winter	
1970 1977	Ernest H. Marsh	
1977 -	Ronald E. F. Dow	

*Nb Tomkynson is not included on the plaque within the Church. He is listed as being Vicar of Dilhorne when sued by Thomas Spener over seizure of cattle on Glebe land at Dilhorne. The dates given are the covering dates of the records of the Court of Star Chamber, and other courts. (National Archives TNA SRAC 2/31/113)

PAGES 125-128 ARE A FEW ENTRIES FOR DILHORNE
IN TRADE DIRECTORIES OVER THE YEARS

DILHORNE, a scattered but pleasant village, 2¼ miles north from Blythe Bridge station, 148 from London, 2½ north-west of Cheadle (comprising within its parish the two townships of FORSBROOK and DILHORNE, supporting their poor conjointly), in the hundred of North Totmonslow, Cheadle union and county court district, Lichfield diocese, Stafford archdeaconry and Cheadle deanery, North Stafford-shire. The living is a vicarage, value £220, with residence, in the incumbency of the Rev. Charles Thomas Dawes, M.A. The Rev. Acton Robert Colvile, B.A., curate; the Marquis of Hastings is the patron. The church of All Saints is an old building, with an heptagon tower and 5 bells; but the nave and aisles were rebuilt in 1819, at an expense of £1,000, and has been repaired in 1859 & 1860 at an expense of about £300. The Wesleyans have a place of worship here Near the church is the Free grammar school, with an income of £261 arising from land. There are also four schools, viz., a girls' and three infant schools, supported by private subscription. There are charities of the yearly value of £8 15s. Dilhorne Hall, the seat of Edward Buller, Esq., is a handsome building, delightfully situate in a valley. Here is also a colliery, about a mile from the village, worked by Mr. Thomas Holmes, who has here a neat residence, com-manding beautiful views of the surrounding country, and the Common colliery worked by Salt and Company. The Hon. Edward Swinfen Jervis is lord of the manor. The population of the parish in 1851 was 1,615, and the acreage is about 3,560.

PRIVATE RESIDENTS

Buller Edward, esq. Hall
Buller Major Coote
Buller Morton Edward, esq
Chell Rev. John, M.A
Colvile Rev. Acton Robert, B.A.[curate]
Stirrup Mrs. Dilhorne house

COMMERCIAL.

Bagnall James, tailor
Bamford James, farmer, Summer hill
Bettany Edward, shopkeeper
Birks Joseph, farmer, Richmond hill
Boulton John, shopkeeper & tailor
Brassington Henry, farmer
Burton John, farmer, New Close fields
Chell Joseph, farmer
Corbishley Joseph, farmer
Eddowes Elijah, farmer, Field house
Eddowes John, butcher
Eddowes William, farmer
Foden Thomas, shoemaker
Hill John, farmer, Whitehurst

Holmes Thomas, coal master, the Elms
Hulme John, master of Free Grammar school
Hunt Thomas, farmer, Tick hill
Inskip Daniel, wheelwright
Inskip Thomas, carpenter & farmer, Mount Pleasant
Jackson Silas, miller & shopkeeper
James William, farmer
Loton Joseph, butcher
Loton John, Holly Bush inn, & black-smith
Malbon Sampson, farmer, Cresswell ford
Mear George, farmer, New hill farm
Mills James, farmer, Stone walls
Moseley Thomas, butcher
Rigby Mary (Mrs.), Colliers' Arms
Salt & Co. coal masters, Dilhorne com-mon colliery
Salt George, shoemaker
Salt John, beer retailer
Salt Joseph, beer retailer, Godley lane

Salt Joseph, *Royal Oak*, & coal master
Salt Priscilla (Mrs.), farmer
Salt Thomas, farmer
Shufflebotham Daniel, farmer, Bank top
Shufflebotham John, farmer, Callow hill
Shufflebotham Loton, farmer, Bank top
Slater Henry, beer retailer
Thorley Enoch, beer retailer
Thorley Michael, farmer, Blake hall
Thorley Elizabeth (Mrs.), farmer, Stansmore hall
Titley John, farmer, New Close fields
Whalley Jonathan, parish clerk & col-lector of property & income taxes
Whitehurst John, farmer
Williamson John, frmr. Haywood grange
Wood John, shoemaker
Wood William, shoemaker
Wright Joseph, farmer, Madge dale
Wright John, butcher, Wetley moor
Wright John, draper & grocer
Letters through Cheadle

Registrar of Births & Deaths, Jonathan Whalley | *Free Grammar School*, John Hulme, master

White's Trade Directory Staffordshire 1854

DILHORNE, or DILHORN, is a small but pleasant village, 2½ miles W.N.W. of Cheadle, and 4 miles E. by N. of Longton, comprising within its parish the townships of Dilhorne and Forsbrook, which support their poor conjointly. The former has 736, and the latter 143 souls, and they contain together about 3550 acres of land. *Dilhorne Hall*, the handsome seat of Edward Buller, Esq., the lord of the manor, stands near the centre of the village, in a romantic dell, and was rebuilt in the ancient style, of brick and stone, about 20 years ago. In the early part of the present century it was the seat of the late John Holiday, Esq., who considerably improved the estate, and planted on it 113,000 mixed timber trees, for which he obtained a gold medal from the Society of Arts. Lady Pilkington, T. H. Parker, Esq., Bamford and Co., and a few smaller owners, have estates here. In the parish are several coal mines. The CHURCH is a large and ancient edifice, dedicated to All Saints; but the nave and aisles were rebuilt in 1819, at the cost of about £1000. The living is a vicarage, valued in K.B. at £8.13s. 1½d., and now at £210, in the patronage of the Dean and Chapter of Lichfield, and incumbency of the Rev. C. T. Dawes, M.A. The Parsonage-house is about to be rebuilt. The patrons are appropriators of the great tithes, which are leased to Mr. Pott, of Chester. The vicar's tithes are commuted for £70 a year. There is a chapel of Ease at Forsbrook, and a Methodist chapel at Godlybrook. Near the church is the *Free Grammar School*, given by one of the vicars, and endowed by one of the Earls of Huntingdon, in the reign of Henry VIII., with 48A. 16P. of land, at Dilhorne; 56A. 3R. 21P. at Caverswall; and 21 acres at Killamarsh, in Derbyshire. This property is now let for £160 per annum, for which the master and usher were required to teach English, writing, arithmetic, &c., to all the children of the parish, but the school is now in Chancery, and the Marquis of Hastings is the trustee. The poor have £8. 15s. yearly, arising from eight small benefactions. Lady Buller supports a girls' school here.

DILHORNE.

Marked 1 are at Bank top; 2, New-close field; and 3 at Whitehurst.
The *Post-office* is at Forsbrook.

Bagnall James, tailor
2 Bamford & Co., coal masters
2 Bamford James, coal master
Bamford Mrs. Hannah, Summer hill
Boucher Rev. Alfred F., A.M., curate of Dilhorne, and incbt. of Forsbrook
Bradbury Sarah, schoolmistress
Buller Edw., Esq., Dilhorne Hall
Buller Morton Edward, Esq., ditto
Chell Jph., maltster; and Rev. John
Dawes Rev. Chas. Thos., M.A., vicar
Eddowes Wm., butcher, &c.
Holmes Thos., coal master, Elms
Hulme John, schoolmaster
Jackson Silas, miller & shopkeeper
1 James John, colliery agent
Inskip Daniel, wheelwright
Loton Jno., smith & vict., Holly Bush
2 Loton Thomas, blacksmith

Mosley Sarah, grocer and draper
Rigby Mary, vict., Colliers' Arms
Salt Jph., shopr. & vict., Royal Oak
Shephard Rev. Hy. Jas., curate of Forsbrook
Thorley Mrs Elizabeth

BOOT & SHOE MKS.	3 Hill John
Foden Thomas	Lockett Samuel
Wood John	Salt Thomas
Whalley Jonathan	1 Shufflebotham
BEERHOUSES.	Dnl. & Isabella
James Edwin	3 Shufflebotham J.
James George	Thorley Thomas
Slater Henry	2 Titley John
FARMERS.	3 Whitehurst Jno.
Bowers Vernon	Williamson John
Corbitchley Jph.	Wright Joseph, &
Carnwell Eliz.	wheelwright

Kelly's Trade Directory Staffordshire 1860

ILHORNE is a parish and scattered but pleasant village, 2½ miles north from Blythe Bridge station, 2½ west om Cheadle, in the Leek division of the county, hundred North Totmonslow, Cheadle union, petty sessional division and county court district, rural deanery of Cheadle, chdeaconry of Stoke-upon-Trent and diocese of Lichfield. he parish comprises the townships of DILHORNE and FORSROOK, the latter being separated for ecclesiastical purposes. he church of All Saints is a building of stone of the twelfth ntury, consisting of chancel, nave, aisles and an octagonal estern tower containing a clock and 5 bells: the nave and sles were rebuilt in 1819, and the entire building repaired 1868 at a cost of about £250: there are 250 sittings. he register dates from the year 1558. The living is a carage, tithe rent-charge £70, gross yearly value £200, cluding 88 acres of glebe, with residence, in the gift of the ean and Chapter of Lichfield, and held since 1883 by the ev. John Beckett, of St. Bees. There is a Wesleyan chapel re. A colliery was opened in this parish in 1884 by essrs. John and Enoch Mann, and is called "Foxfield olliery." The charities are of the yearly value of about 30. Dilhorne Hall, the seat of Sir Morton Edward Manngham-Buller bart. B.A., D.L., J.P. is a handsome building,

delightfully situated in a valley. The Hon. Edward Swynfen Parker-Jervis, of Little Aston Hall, Stonnall, who is lord of the manor, Sir Morton Edward Manningham-Buller bart. and Sir Lionel Milborne Swinnerton-Pilkington bart. D.L. of Chevet Hall, near Wakefield, are the chief landowners. The soil is principally clay; subsoil, the same. The crops are all kinds of cereals. The area of the parish is 3,769 acres of land and 7 of water; rateable value, £8,365; the population in 1881 was 1,637.

BOUNDARY and DAISY BANK, both about 1 mile south-east, are villages in this parish.

Parish Clerk, Richard Hurst.

POST OFFICE.—James Bagnall, sub-postmaster. Letters arrive from Stoke-on-Trent at 7.30 a.m.; dispatched at 6.20 p.m. Nearest money order office is at Blythe Bridge & telegraph office at Cheadle

Mixed Schools, under the management of governors, in part appointed under a scheme drawn up by the Endowed Schools Commission, were erected in 1876 at a cost of £2,000, being a part of the funds raised from the sale of property belonging to the old school; the school will hold 150 children; average attendance, 105; Thomas Chadwick, master; Miss Mary Black, assistant mistress

PRIVATE RESIDENTS.

eckett Rev. John [vicar]
oote Henry St. George, The Elms
and Thomas, Blakeley house
ckson Bertram, The Elms
oton Miss
anningham-Buller Sir Morton Edward bart. B.A., D.L., J.P. Dilhorne hall
iller Dugald Stewart, Dilhorne house
alt Charles
mith Mrs
ackland John
right John

COMMERCIAL.

agnall James, tailor, draper & grocer, Post office
eardmore Henry, farmer
ettany William, farmer
ettany William, farmer, Stansmore hall
ettany William, farmer, Dilhorne com
randrick Charles, farmer, Stonewalls
orbishley Joseph, farmer, Dilhorne Hill farm
arnwell Enoch, registrar of births & deaths for Dilhorne sub-district &

vaccination officer for Dilhorne & Cheadle sub-districts, Cheadle union, Godley brook
Docksey Ephraim, farmer, Newclose frm
Dunn George, farmer, Summer hill
Forrester George, farmer
Forrester Joseph, farmer
Foxfield Colliery (John & Enoch Mann, proprietors)
Fynney Richard, farmer, Malthouse frm
Heath John, farmer, Bank Top
Hill George, farmer, Whitehurst
Hunt Matthew, farmer, Tick hill
Inskip Frederick Thomas, builder, timber merchant, brickmaker & inspector of nuisances to Cheadle rural sanitary authority
Loton George, farmer & blacksmith
Loton Mary (Miss), cowkeeper
Makepeace John, head gardener to Sir M. E. Manningham-Buller bart. D.L., J.P
Martin Samuel, farmer, Newclose fields
Mellor John, farmer, Old Engine farm
Moseley Rupert, butcher & cattle dealer, Dilhorne common

Moseley Thomas, butcher & farmer
Morris Abraham Alfred, beer retailer, Boundary
Plant William, farmer, Blake hall
Salt Herbert, Royal Oak P.H. & farmer
Salt John, blacksmith
Salt John, tea dealer, Boundary
Salt Joseph, beer retailer, Godley brook
Salt Margaret (Mrs.), beer rtlr. Boundary
Shenton Ephraim, farmer, Field house
Shoebotham Arthur, farmer, Bank top
Shoebotham Daniel, farmer, Bank top
Shoebotham John, farmer
Shoebotham Loton, farmer, Whitehurst
Shoebotham Sarah (Mrs.), farmer, Callow hill
Ward Andrew, farmer, Haywood grange
Warrington Wm. farmer, Adderley frm
Whitehurst James, farmer & assistant. overseer, St. Thomas' trees
Whitehurst Emma (Mrs.), farmer
Wright Joseph, farmer, Mount Pleasant
Wright Samson, Colliers Arms P.H. & farmer

Kelly's Trade Directory Staffordshire 1888

DILHORNE.

DILHORNE PARISH COUNCIL.

Chairman.—James M. Brassington.

Clerk.—J. Beardmore.

Postal Address.—Dilhorne : Nr. Blythe Bridge, Stoke-on-Trent.

Overseers' Names and Addresses.—J. M. Brassington, W. J. Thorley, Dilhorne.

Population.—700.

Local Member of Cheadle Rural District Council.—J. T. Mear.

Nearest Railway Station—Blythe Bridge (N.S.R.)

ALPHABETICAL DIRECTORY.

Beardmore, Joseph, poor rate collector, Dilhorne Common
Bentley, E., Rose and Crown, (B.H.), Godley Brook
Bettany, Edward, farmer, Dilhorne Common
Bettany, Wm., farmer, Dilhorne Common
Bishop, W., farmer, Whitehurst
Brassington, William, Whitehurst
Burden, R., Blakeley House
Carnwell, Hannah, Godley Brook
Chadwick, Thomas, Mastin
Challinor, Charles, farmer
Challinor, William, farmer, Godley-lane
Clewlow, Charles, farmer
Clowes, Albert, farmer, Cresswell Ford
Edwards, Samuel, farmer, New Hill
Foster, Thomas, farmer, Blakehall

Fletcher, Ephraim, farmer, Newclose Fields
Foxfield Colliery Company, Foxfield
Foxley, Saml., farmer, Malthouse
Goodwin, John, farmer, Richmond Hill
Harrison, Chas., grocer and corn seller
Harrison, James, farmer, Newclose Fields
Heath, Daniel, Stone Walls
Heath, John, farmer, Bank Top
Hulme, Wm., farmer, Mount Pleasant
Loton, Mary, farmer
Makepeace, Jno., Beech House
Mear, James, Dilhorne House
Mear, W. F.
Mears, Arthur, farmer, Above Park
Moore, Edwin, John, Wetley Moor
Mosley, Thos. and Sons, butchers and farmers
Parfitt, John, Dilhorne Common
Parr, James, farmer
Plant, Rev. G. R., The Vicarage
Prestwood, H., farmer
Radford, John W., Colliers' Arms (F.L.)
Shelley, John, Royal Oak (F.L.)
Slack, Thomas, farmer, Summer Hill
Smith, I. J., foreman
Stephenson, Jno., colliery manager, Godley-lane
Stones, T. W., farmer, Gallow Hill
Thorley, Edwin, Old Engine
Thorley, Thomas, Godley Brook
Timmis, Thomas, Whitehurst
Warner, W., farmer, Haywood Grange
Wheat, Charles, Adderley Farm
Whitehurst, Fred, Whitehurst
Whitehurst, Joseph, St. Thomas Trees

Newcastle & District Trade Directory 1912

DILHORNE is a parish and scattered but pleasant village, 2 miles north from Blythe Bridge station on the Stoke and Uttoxeter section of the London, Midland and Scottish railway, 2½ west from Cheadle, in the Stone division of the county, hundred of North Totmonslow, rural district, petty sessional division and rural deanery of Cheadle, archdeaconry of Stoke-upon-Trent and diocese of Lichfield. The church of All Saints is a building of stone of the 12th century, consisting of chancel, nave, aisles and an octagonal western tower containing a clock and 5 bells : the nave and aisles were rebuilt in 1819, and the entire building repaired in 1868 : in 1885 a new organ was added and various improvements effected : the church contains four stained windows, three of them memorials : a baptistery was completed in 1922, a donation for the purpose being made by Sir William Thorley Loton, of Perth, Western Australia, who was born in the parish in 1839 : there are 280 sittings. The register dates from the year 1558.

The living is a vicarage, net yearly value £350, with residence, in the gift of the Dean and Chapter of Lichfield, and held since 1929 by the Rev. St. John Guy Maule Vernon, of Lichfield Theological College. There is a Wesleyan chapel here. Foxfield colliery, in this parish, was opened in 1884 by Messrs. John and Enoch Mann. The charities are of the yearly value of about £24. Lt.-Col. William Swynfen Whitehall Parker-Jervis D.S.O. who is lord of the manor, and Lady Feilden are the chief landowners. The soil is principally clay ; subsoil, the same. The crops are all kinds of cereals. The area of the parish is 2,476 acres of land and 2 of water ; the population of the civil parish in 1921 was 687, and of the ecclesiastical parish, 828.

Post, M. O. & Tel. Call Office. Letters from Stoke-on-Trent. Blythe Bridge nearest T. office

PRIVATE RESIDENTS.

(For T N's see general list of Private Residents at end of book.)

(Marked thus † letters should be addressed Cheadle, Stoke.)

Bassett Ralph Hall, Blakeley house
†Dixon Charles Huntley, The Elms
Harris John Elvine, The Old Vicarage
Plant Mrs. Alice, Carfax
Vernon Rev. St. John Guy Maule (vicar), Vicarage

COMMERCIAL.

Marked thus ° farm 150 acres or over.

Beardmore Jsph. Colliers' Arms P.H
Bentley Michael, farmer, St. Thomas' trees
Bettany Edward, farmer
Blood Wm. J. Royal Oak P.H
Blurton Wm. farmer, Whitehurst frm

Brassington Hannah & Eliz. (Mrs.), farmers, Whitehurst
°Brown Wm. farmer, Stansmore hall
Champ Jn. Wm. frmr. Wardhill frm
Dale Enoch, shopkpr. Post office. T N Blythe Bridge 99
Edwards Wm. farmer, Newhill
Fenton Geo. & Ethel (Miss), farmers, Malthouse
Goodwin John, farmer, Richmond hill
Goodwin Thomas, frmr. Mt. Pleasant
Gould Alfd. farmer, Summerhill
†Harrison Jas. farmer, Newclose fields
Harvey Wm. farmer, Blakehall farm
Hughes Charles, frmr. Cresswell ford
Jackson Reuben, farmer, Madgedale
Johnson Thos. farmer
Leese William, farmer, Overmoor, Cellarhead
Massey Arth. farmer, Newclose fields
Mear Fredk. Wm. farmer, Bank top. T N Wetley Rocks 18
Mear George, farmer, Bank Top

Moreton Thomas, farmer, Overmoor, Cellarhead
Mosley Arth. farmer, Dayhouse
Oakley Rt. milk seller, Church farm
Park Hall Collieries Co. Ltd. coal owners, Foxfield colliery. T N Cheadle 83
†Pegg Ernest, farmer, Adderley farm
Sales Walter, beer ret. Godley brook
Sammons Chas. A. farmer, Dilhorne common
°Slack Thos. & Sons, farmers, Heywood grange
Spooner Fredk. farmer, The Croft
Thorley Jesse, frmr. Old Engine frm
Tompkin Clement, farmer, Home frm
Turnock Wilmot, farmer, Stonewalls
Twigg Wm. farmer, Mount Pleasant
Urion Fredk. Danl. farmer, Dilhorne House farm
Wheat Ernest, farmer, Whitehurst
Whitehurst Joseph, farmer, St. Thomas' trees

Kelly's Trade Directory Staffordshire 1932